A Celebration of Cats

A Celebration

Roger A. Caras

Robson Books

First published in Great Britain in 1989 by Robson Books Ltd,
Bolsover House, 5–6 Clipstone Street, London W1P 7EB

British Library Cataloguing in Publication Data
Caras, Roger A. (Roger Andrew, 1928–   )
  A celebration of cats.
  1. Cats
  I. Title
  636.8

ISBN 0 86051 591 5

Printed in Great Britain by
St Edmundsbury Press Ltd, Bury St Edmunds, Suffolk

Acknowledgments

Is there a new way of saying thank you to all the people who always help make any book possible? If there is, I haven't discovered it. Jill, my wife of thirty-two years, has rejoiced in each of our cats with me, and suffered the loss of each in turn when that time came. Phyllis Langdon Barclay (my mother-in-law of thirty-two years, by some coincidence) has made it possible for us to maintain our herd and travel at the same time. It just would not have been possible without her. Dee, our housekeeper for considerably less than thirty-two years, has certainly done more than her share and has spent more time with various vacuum systems than most people spend eating each day. George Dwyer, who isn't even thirty-two, has kept me, my obligations and this manuscript on track with an iron fist. And to all of our cat-owning friends who have shared their views and news on matters feline with us, enduring gratitude. As for you, the cats we have known, I tried to learn, truly I did. In a way this book is a test of your combined skills at educating a human being.

This book is dedicated in bewildered gratitude to Michael, Thai-Lin, Abigail, Eartha Kat, Meep, Daisy, Kate the Good, Omari, Maridadi, Mr. Amanda, Xnard, Squid, Jackie, Livia Augusta, Ping, Rufus, Pansy, Poppy, Shasta, Mouse, Mitten, Lucy Sugar, Emily, Walter, Wong, Kiko, Pickles, Fidel, Clothild, Safari, Siafu and all of the others. Every one was a friend and teacher, and not one was independent, aloof or any of the other silly things cats are said to be. They were all closet smoochers.

*Studies for the fifty-three stages of the Tokaido,
by Kuniyoshi, c. 1848*

Contents

Foreword

PEOPLE WHO have never owned cats (cats don't own people, that is a misinterpretation of a splendid relationship) or who do not know how to relate to cats often say that cats are independent, that they don't need us, that they deign to share our homes with us out of wisdom, generosity or some other characteristic that is clearly human and not at all feline. I like a splash of anthropomorphism when discussing my pets as well as anyone, but these seemingly mandatory comments on cats are to me so much dreary nonsense.

If a cat could be wise, it would be, I am certain. If a cat could deign, I am certain a great many of them would, because cats are amazingly adept at working out relationships. If cats are aloof and independent I can't for the life of me figure out what has been climbing, leaping and crawling into my lap through all of my childhood and adult years. Of all the cats we Carases have ever owned, one small, sad gray animal, Willie, an under-the-sofa croucher, was the only one who never came around. He was our single failure. Every other cat that has ever been invited to join our thundering herd of cats, dogs and people has figured the thing out. They have all craved attention and learned how to extract it. It is a very simple formula, really. To get attention you give it. Cats engage in social grooming. They nuzzle you so that you will nuzzle them back, or at least pat them. At the same time they are marking you with what is to us an invisible scent of possession, a pheromone detectable only to cats.

On cold evenings our cats curl up with our dogs, particularly but not exclusively the larger dogs because they are such efficient heat conductors. On hot evenings our cats know which windows bring the breezes and where the flow of air from the whirring ceiling fans is most rewarding. Even though they do not have perspiration to evaporate and therefore cool them, they like a bit of cool air in the evening, preferably in motion. Cats are, after all (and so to speak), hedonistic materialists. On any evening they know which laps are most promising and which chins and cheeks to nuzzle for maximum return per push. They are no more intelligent than dogs (though surely *as* intelligent), but they have transcended whatever their original lack of social grace may have been, something the wolf-descended dogs never had to do since wolves were and are very social animals. Dogs, God love them, come with social mechanisms built in. Of all wildcat species, only the lion has a social unit, and lions had no part in forming our domestic cat. But all is not lost. Any cat properly socialized as a kitten and well cared for as an adult is intelligent enough to work out a system to gain the advantages that dogs gain almost automatically.

We have developed strong clichés about many of the

animals with which we have had long-term experience. Elephants never forget, bulls are aggressive, ants are industrious, foxes are sly, dogs are loyal, horses are strong and faithful, sheep follow anything anywhere (that is almost true), lions are majestic, snakes are slimy, coyotes are tricksters, owls are wise, rats are dirty, bats get in your hair, and cats are aloof and independent users. Those generally intolerably anthropomorphic generalizations work out about as well as ethnic characterizations of human races, religions and nationalities. Some cats are aloof, but so are some dogs. Some cats are independent, but so are some horses. (It is true that foxes know how to survive when the odds are against them, but "sly" goes too far. Owls look like they should be wise but I know of no evidence to support such a claim; to me they look startled or at least amazed.)

What cats are is individualistic. One of their most enchanting traits is that each one you meet really does require meeting. Expect what you want, anticipate what you will, a new cat will still force you to make your way with it into a whole new relationship. The chances are you will get as much out of it as you are willing to put into it. A great deal of it will be unpredictable, and just about all of it (assuming you and the cat can make out together, by no means a certainty) will be a pleasure. In the pages that follow we will attempt to analyze and celebrate the individualism and pleasure of cats. But first set aside your prejudices, pro as well as con. We will seek all that the cat really is, the one that ate the rat, the one that laughed at Alice, the one that visited the queen. No one is more intriguing than any other, all of them are living out our fantasies. We live in part through them, they in part through us. It has been a reasonably long—about four thousand years—and very complicated relationship. It is the stuff of which art and poetry are made, and not just a few of our dreams.

Book illustration by Steinlen, 19th century

1
Ailurophiles, Ailurophobes

TRADITION HAS IT that Adolf Hitler hated cats. He probably did; everything else was wrong with him. Napoleon also hated cats. There are endlessly repeated stories about the French emperor and his problem. On one occasion, it is said, he was heard calling hoarsely for help from his tent. Aides rushed in expecting to find an assassin at work and found Napoleon alone instead, sword drawn, doing battle with the rich tapestry hangings he enjoyed having around him. He insisted he had either seen or could sense a cat lurking somewhere behind them. He was gasping for breath, red in the face, near collapse. He had to be helped to his bed, and a doctor was called in to settle him down. How much of that is just more Napoleonic lore, of which there is a great deal, and how much truth is difficult to determine, but clearly the man who would conquer the world could not overcome an unreasoning dread of a small, harmless companion animal.

It is interesting that Napoleon and Hitler shared this fear, because a third would-be conqueror of the world, Alexander the Great, is supposed to have been numbered among the world's premier ailurophobes as well. It is said that he would swoon at the sight of cat. Fearless before armies, indifferent to personal danger, the man who legend says wept because there were no more nations to conquer, no more armies to annihilate, was terrified of a house cat.

What is there about the cat that so threatens, or perhaps frustrates, world conquerors? Perhaps it is that cats are difficult to conquer. Although easy to kill, they are hard to dominate. And so, perhaps deep in our psyches, cats represent the unconquerable. The less than admirable Henry III of France hated cats and so did Napoleon's biographer Hilaire Belloc (who could never decide whether he should be French or English—indeed, he seems to have been confused about a lot of things). The composer Meyerbeer was also said to be a cat hater, which is strange for a creative artist. The critics gave his operas a very bad time when they were first performed, so perhaps Meyerbeer needed a scapecat. Obviously something was wrong.

But look at the other column, the far more benevolent, less frustrated people who have loved cats. Anne Frank and Victor Hugo (to establish a spread), Edgar Allan Poe and Mark Twain, Paul Gallico and Lewis Carroll, Jules Verne, George Bernard Shaw, and Aesop, Pierre Bonnard the artist, Erté the designer, Ogden Nash the humorist (despite his nasty little poem "The trouble with a kitten is that/Eventually it becomes a cat"). All were cat lovers by declaration or reasonable inference. T. S. Eliot for certain was a cat admirer as were Thomas Hardy and J. R. R. Tolkien. James Thurber is on the list, as are Dr. Johnson and Mark van Doren, Stuart Cloete and Budd Schulberg. Harriet Beecher Stowe, Adlai Stevenson and William Rossetti were wise enough to appreciate if not adore cats. (They probably adored them, but I can't prove it.) Renoir, Courbet, Manet and P. G. Wodehouse—all part of the great international circle of cat-loving intellectuals, artists and authors.

H. H. Munro, under his pen name Saki, nearly frightened me to death with his story "The Monkey's Paw" (I was about ten), but I forgave him because of his affection for cats. Beatrix Potter never frightened me, but she loved cats, too, as did Baudelaire and Edward Lear. Sir Walter Scott had a bit of trouble with cats, strangely enough. He was always devoted to very unfeline Scottish deerhounds (the "fairest creatures of heaven," I think he called them), and as a young man he was not really keen on cats, but eventually, as he matured and his mind improved, he came around and actually ended up apologizing for his earlier failing. He died a devoted cat person. Other admirers include Walter De La Mare, W. B. Yeats, Ernest Hemingway, John Keats, Alexandre Dumas, Theodore Roosevelt, William Carlos Williams, Booth Tarkington, Colette, Ambrose Bierce, Henry David Thoreau (of course). Maurice Ravel had between thirty and forty cats. Mary Queen of Scots's son, James I of England (who was also James VI of Scotland), the successor to Elizabeth I, was a big cat lover. Abraham Lincoln kept four cats in the White House. Evidently cats have often been close to the seat of power.

Clearly, the list is impressively diverse and satisfyingly replete with the good as well as the famous.

I mentioned James I in passing and we should return there for just a moment. Not only did his predecessor on the throne, Elizabeth I, have James's mother beheaded (I have never accepted the theory that she didn't mean to do it. It seems to me that cutting someone's head off is a pretty definite statement and not one that is likely to occur by carelessness with one's signature), but she was really awful to cats. To emphasize how much "Good Queen Bess" disliked people of the Roman faith, she had a wicker pope made for her own coronation, and then had this large and unusual effigy stuffed (or at least permitted it to be) with living cats and set on fire so that the screams of the burning cats would mock "popery" and Rome. It is not clear whether Elizabeth herself set the thing ablaze or had it done for her while she watched, but as we shall encounter in another chapter, it was nothing unusual around that time. Even so, despite a grudging admiration for her on other grounds, I have never really forgiven Elizabeth that bit of brutality. I have always taken it worse than I have Mary's abrupt conclusion after all those years in Elizabeth's prisons.

Now Mary's grandson, Charles II, was a good enough fellow and he did love animals. I am sure he didn't participate in the bad handling of cats that continued after the time of Elizabeth and cut down on urban ratting efficiency, which may in turn have contributed to the outbreaks of plague a little later on. Cats have their ways of getting even.

The centuries of the cat's mistreatment have come down to us in scraps, and with that sorry history has come a lot of nonsense about the cat as an untrustworthy, even malicious, creature, nonsense that has undoubtedly contributed to a good deal of ailurophobia, the pathological fear of cats. There have been stories of malevolent cats strangling their masters alive. In 1809 a schoolmaster whose name is happily forgotten published a book called *Natural History for Children*. In it he says of the cat:

> . . . the cat is a very false and faithless and thievish
> animal which neither by caresses and good feeling nor by

blows and imprisonment can be so tamed that it will not scratch and steal. It is and remains always a malignant deceiver.

Hardly less zoologically accurate was Dr. Ludwig Jerrer, who in 1833 published *Natural History for the Young*, and it states:

> You know what a flattering, snuggling but also false, spiteful, faithless animal the housecat is. How it scratches and bites and robs and steals! There is no worse thief than the cat. . . . For that reason many people cannot endure it, and some find cats so repellent to their natures that they fall in a faint if a cat so much as comes close to them.

The nonsense went back and forth unabated. Cats adored, cats despised, cats honored and cats abused—there never was any reason for any of it. Can ailurophobia be cured? Maybe not in the days of Alexander or even Napoleon, but it can be cured today as, I am sure, can any phobia.

Not very long ago my wife, Jill, and I had a dinner at the home of editor Eleanor Friede. Eleanor, who is a pilot and does lots of other neat, independent things, was the publishing executive who got Richard Bach to finish *Jonathan Livingston Seagull* and single-handedly got the thing published against all advice and thereby made everybody rich. Besides editing and flying and entertaining most graciously, Eleanor loves cats. Sitting next to me at dinner was a charming woman, and when one of Eleanor's many cats jumped into her lap the woman began patting it.

"A year ago, if a cat had jumped into my lap, I would have fainted," she said. "I might have required hospitalization."

She went on to explain that her husband had always loved cats as much as she despised them. You really couldn't blame her since they made her swoon just by walking across the room. When her kids announced they loved cats, too,

A Persian pottery cat, 13th century

and her whole family ganged up on her about getting a cat, she had to give in. It was decided that they would get the smallest kitten possible. If this woman had the little thing growing up in her care, surely she would get used to it before she had a chance to become terrified of it. It seemed to make sense, but it didn't.

"When my husband went to work and the kids went to school I was alone in our apartment with the tiny thing and I just couldn't stand it. I could feel my skin crawling. I went out into Central Park and sat on a bench feeling like a perfect idiot until the kids came home from school to save me. I couldn't sleep nights, knowing it was there. I began to lose weight and I walked around all day, away from the apartment, as if I were in a trance. After a while my husband realized what was going on and the cat went. I quickly became normal again—respectably terrified of all cats."

But things did not go back to normal. Eleanor's house guest now lay awake at night trying to think through her totally unreasonable behavior. On her own, without saying anything to her family, she went to a psychiatrist. She saw him four times, she underwent hypnosis, and now cats can jump into her lap at Eleanor's house.

Any case of ailurophobia is curable, as long as the person wants to be cured and isn't working the story up to attract attention. (We had a friend who leaped off couches, screamed, turned her face to the wall and started sobbing when a cat walked into the room. I never knew how much was ailurophobia, how much genuine pathology, and how much of the performance, in the woman's own view, made her interesting. She was highly suspect.) Less subject to modification, unfortunately, are allergies.

It is not cat hair that causes people's eyes to go red, their noses to run and their throats to threaten to clamp shut, cutting off their air supply. The villain is cat dander, and while a brisk daily brushing administered by a nonallergic friend or family member will cut down on the dander-covered hair cats generally leave around, something more is needed. Dr. Louis Camuti, a New York veterinarian, specialized in cats alone for fifty years. He didn't have a clinic but only made house calls (he wrote a couple of delightful books, one of which is called *All My Patients Are Under the Bed*) and these calls he made at night.

Dr. Camuti would get up at three in the afternoon, have breakfast, and take phone calls until six, when he and his wife set out on their rounds. Mrs. Camuti would wait in the car, to intercept parking tickets, and Dr. Camuti would visit his patients, every kind from Russian blues in a Park Avenue penthouse to a nondescript random-bred in an artist's loft in Greenwich Village. The Camutis usually got home at six in the morning, when they would have dinner and go to bed.

I once spent a night doing their rounds with them. Clearly, the doctor loved cats. Yet back at his house the next morning there wasn't a cat to be seen. I asked how this was so for a veterinarian who had refused to deal with any animal besides the cat for half a century. He answered very simply, "I'm allergic to them." It was true. Every evening before heading out on his appointed rounds, Dr. Camuti shot up with antihistamines, big doses of the stuff. And he lived to be well past eighty years old. Allergies to cats can all but rule them out of your life. It is a shame.

What is this animal that it would be a shame to be alienated from? All of those great writers I listed earlier in our partial catalog of cat lovers have described the cat. In the seventeenth century Edward Topsall said, "A cat is a watchful and warye beast, sildome overtaken, and most attendant to her sport and prey." Topsall's spelling notwithstanding, cats *are* wary and watchful. That is accurate enough.

In the last century, A. C. Swinburne wrote:

> *Stately, kindly lordly friend*
> *Condescend*
> *Here to sit by me, and turn*
> *Glorious eyes that smile and burn,*
> *Golden eyes, love's lustrous meed,*
> *On the golden page I read.*

Not too bad, that, and hear Thomas Gray in the eighteenth century:

> *Her conscious tail her joy declared,*
> *The fair round face, the snowy beard,*
> *The velvet of her paws,*
> *Her coat, that with the tortoise views,*
> *Her ears of jet, and emerald eyes,*
> *She saw; and purr'd applause.*

Unfortunately, Gray's own puss drowned in a tub of goldfish that she had been eying, with no good in mind, I am sure. Cats do that. They are clever but they still manage to get in the most terrible fixes.

So just in those two quotes out of the thousands available to us, we have an animal that is wary, watchful, stately, lordly, has glorious eyes and velvet paws and is, by all possible definitions, beautiful.

There are endless tales of cats refusing to acknowledge monarchs as anything but people, and therein we have one of the cat's principal appeals: it is a great equalizer. Cats bring us all down to a common level where, perhaps, most of us belong. There is no way you can impress a cat. It is not as if cats sneer at us: it is that cats have perspective, they have things pulled together, and they are impeccably well orga-

nized as they sit and watch the charade acted out. Cats seem
to know the punch lines of life. They know how the play will
end, so they make themselves comfortable and wait it out.
They have tempers and passions, they get hungry, and they
are very lusty sexually, but all of those things seem to be
diversions. They know what is important and when to expect important things to happen. In the meantime, they can
play with a mouse, dawdle with a bit of fluff, or whack at a
wooden spool dangled by a bit of thread, or they can just wait,
paws to breast. They like warm places, but they are very,
very "cool" in the way many teen-agers like to be cool. (The
ultimate compliment in our recent vernacular is to call
someone a "cool cat.") These all are traits most people
would want to have said about themselves, even people with
allergies.

I should think it really impossible to describe the cat
because, among other things, you have to be subjective,
whether you admit it or not. You are also reacting to the cats
you have known. There is no way that you can be objective.
If you are allergic to cat dander and nearly strangle in the
presence of the beasts, or if you are afflicted with untreated
ailurophobia and have found yourself on the verge of losing
consciousness in the presence of a cat, you are not going to
react like Dr. Johnson, who apparently almost always had one
clamped to his bosom, or like anyone else for whom cats were
the dearest companions of all. My daughter, Pamela, had
three successive cats as a child, and each slept on her pillow
and listened to all her secrets. She will see cats very differently
from that man who was willing to kill absolutely any number
of people in order to control the world. How then, without
being silly and subjective, define or describe the cat? One way
is to describe how people have behaved toward the cat. We
will get to that in later chapters, but we can steal a quick look

ahead, before we turn our attention next to the question of where this puzzling animal came from.

People have worshiped cats. They have embalmed cats and kept their preserved bodies as shrines. They have painted and drawn cats hundreds of thousands of times, often extremely well. Such paintings appeared in China and Japan and Thailand, at the French court, in stately English mansions, in Italy, and on ancient pottery and in even more ancient friezes. There have been volumes of poetry written about cats, and cats have figured in literature from the beginning of fiction. Cats have been tortured and burned, slaughtered and blamed for almost all the ills of man. Cats have been accused of being witches, or at least working for witches. They have been said to be vampires. In short, almost all extremes of human rage, adoration, religious ecstasy, and creativity have been focused on cats. None of this is explicable unless you know the cat itself. Let's try for that.

Study by Kuniyoshi

Ceramic figure of a cat,
Japanese, Middle Jomon period (c. 1750 B.C.)

2
Probable
Beginnings

FIVE OF OUR earth's seven present continents have been inhabited by true cats for at least forty million years. Only Antarctica and Australia have been isolated for so long that they were left out when our planet's allotment of cats was distributed. Africa got the lion, the leopard, the cheetah, the serval, and a kind of lynx known as the caracal. Asia also got the lion and the leopard, the tiger, and both the clouded and snow leopard in limited areas. Europe got the lion, too. North and South America (including Central America) got the mountain lion or puma (or cougar or panther or painter—it has lots of names) and the jaguar (called, confusingly, *el tigre* in Latin America), the jaguarundi, ocelot, and margay. North America got, as well, two cousins, the bobcat and the lynx.

Spread across all of this vast global range, there has also

been a veritable tangle of small wildcats known by scores of scientific and popular names. They belong now to the genus *Felis*, and although scientists once put more than two hundred and thirty animals in the genus, it is now down to a more workable twenty-five to twenty-eight species. By no means has the last word been heard on the subject, though. The taxonomy, or scientific naming and associating of the small wildcats, remains a muddle and a mystery. We should do no more than nod at it or we will be drawn in and suffocate without coming to any conclusions. There is a whole mess, then, of small wildcats, many of them barely larger than puss-by-the-fire. Most have about the same markings and colors—what we call "tabby"—as the majority of domestic cats. Keep in mind that there are undoubtedly more extinct species of cats than extant. We are speaking here about what is left. All kinds of marvelous creatures like the saber-toothed cat, or *Smilodon*, are long gone. (I have a lovely cast of a *Smilodon* skull. That was quite a cat!)

Now we are going to have to stay with this for a moment if we hope to arrive at some approximation of the original domestic cat. There is a North African wildcat which many scientists say is a subspecies—as some scientists would have it—of a rather more northern European wildcat. Hence, in Europe, there is *Felis silvestris silvestris*, and in Asia Minor, southern Asia, and northern Africa, there is *Felis silvestris libyca*. The latter has the same first and second names, but a different third name from its European cousin, which means it is a *sub*species. Other scientists, just as concerned with knowing the facts, say "not so." They point to *Felis silvestris* up north and *Felis libyca* farther south and give the North African job a species designation all its own—whichever label they prefer. However, just about all scientists agree that the little tabbylike wildcat from North Africa—whether *Felis sil-*

vestris libyca or *Felis libyca*—was the primary ancestor of the domestic animal going under the rather late Latin name of *catus*. In many ways, *catus* has changed dramatically since coming under man's domestic care, but in other ways it often seems to be marking time.

Domestication probably started in Egypt around four thousand years ago but it is impossible to be absolutely certain; bones of domestic cats and small wildcats are extremely difficult to distinguish from one another. In fact, domestication can be far easier to establish by the archeological circumstances in which the bones are discovered than by the bones themselves. Over the years, a lot of people have written about the mixes the emerging *Felis catus* was subjected to. They have said that *Felis libyca* (or *Felis silvestris libyca*) mixed with *Felis silvestris silvestris* farther north, inasmuch as the early domestic cats lived tramplike lives (they still will if we let them) and bred with anything that seemed right at the time, or was simply handy. That is probably correct. The domestic cat, pretty much an Egyptian idea as far as we know, moved north into Europe at a steady rate once Christianity replaced the Egyptian pantheon and the cat was no longer sacred. Apparently the god-state is a profound social inhibitor—but that gets us ahead of ourselves. Let's first take care of those possible or probable mixes.

In central Asia there is a wildcat known as the steppe cat, a tough little denizen of rocky, semi-arid areas and a terrific nocturnal hunter. Its name is *Felis manul*. A lot of people have said that *F. manul* interbred and produced what we call the Persian longhaired cat. Probably not so. The longhaired trait in our domestic cat was almost certainly a much later development achieved by fine breeding of our already solidly companion animal. Then there is another wildcat found in Egypt, a fierce little predator, that ranges east to Sri Lanka

Case for a mummified cat, Egyptian

and India and many other areas as well. It is called the jungle
cat, *Felis chaus*, but again, it probably is not an ancestor of
our lap-sitting friend. Maybe there was a small degree of
cross-pollination, so to speak, for it must be remembered that
cats are highly sexual animals. A queen in heat wants action
right then and there, and any males nearby are not only at-
tracted but determined to do their part. No one can possibly
say that a little *F. manul* or *F. chaus* didn't sneak in along the

way, but it wasn't something that happened often enough, certainly not with intent by cat owners, to earn those other wildcats that stripe of ancestors. Friend of the family, perhaps, but not really ancestor.

Still, some confusion about the Egyptian mix remains, given the Egyptian habit of mummifying their dead cats by the thousands along with other pets, including wild animals that got taken into homes or private zoos as small creatures and grew up fairly socialized if not actually domesticated. Mummified *Felis chaus* bones, along with those of other species, have shown up along with bones of what appear to have been domesticated cats, leading to the probably erroneous conclusion that they were all together in one mix. After all, if you kept a full-blooded wolf as a pet or curiosity (and the Egyptians were devoted to curiosities, animal and human), and when it died you buried it near your old German shepherd dog and your mastiff, you could lay the same kind of trap for future scientists that apparently was inadvertently laid down by the Egyptians well before the time of Christ. Taxonomy can be a very hazardous pastime, with so many dead ends, and most scientists, once ensnared, find a U-turn more than their egos can manage.

Not only is the Egyptian mix questionable; it is even uncertain that Egypt was the very first place where the domestic cat was purposefully bred. In the oldest known city in the world, Jericho, near the Dead Sea and well northeast of Egypt, there was some kind of cat-and-man association during the pre-pottery Neolithic age, about 7000 B.C. There are a few other such distracting beacons, but none of them clearly involve what we can in all fairness call domestic cats. Still, at any of these points there could have been some species of *Felis* besides our adored *catus*, and some tribes of man toying with the idea of the cat.

One of the factors that points to Egypt does not involve bones but grain. The silo was an Egyptian invention during the Eighteenth Dynasty of the New Kingdom, roughly in the sixteenth century B.C. There probably wasn't a specific silo inventor—the silo was almost surely a case of rapid evolution —but however it originated, it coincided with the first apparent appearance of the domestic cat. There's an obvious connection: silos are where you store grain, and stored grain attracts rats and mice in large numbers. Rats and mice in concentrated populations certainly attract cats, both wild and domestic, and if the line between the two kinds of cat were to become obscured, as with the very process of domestication, it would logically occur where silos appeared for the first time on earth. (If you stick with any aspect of cats long enough, a certain ineffable logic emerges. You may have to be as patient as a cat waiting by a mouse hole for the first glimpse of a whisker, but inevitably the logic will appear.)

The wildcats that would have begun creeping around the first crude silos at night listening for the skitter and scurry of rodent feet would have been striped tabbies, and that almost certainly was the color and design of the first domestic cats. Man's relatively short history of living with the domestic cat has not been anywhere near as economically motivated as his association with other animals that have entered his fold and were domesticated long before the silo's invention—dogs as herders and guards, cattle, horses, camels, water buffalo, pigs, sheep and goats, fowl and a few others. But in those early Egyptian days cats were undeniably useful as ratters and mousers. You could say that the better mousetrap had been invented. It probably bit and scratched, back that close to its wild origins, and it was strangely aloof compared to the dogs that had already been around for a long, long time, but it was good on rodents and it purred when it was happy.

Prehistoric carving of a cat,
French, Magdalenian IV

The cat was probably not the only wild animal kept in captivity and selectively bred at that time as a mouser. Two others were good enough with rats and mice to earn the same attention: the ferret and the mongoose. Both are still found in captivity, still doing the same work, with the mongoose serving double duty where cobras and the like are a bother. But it was the cat that caught our fancy and has come forward in time to become one of our two foremost companion animals.

Cat retrieving ducks, Egyptian

I'm not exactly certain why, but it has been suggested that even before the New Kingdom and the silo, cats may have been used as retrievers. I include that bit of dubious intelligence only because it is potentially good trivia, but I doubt that anyone will ever be able to prove it. The suggestion does crop up, and since it is one of the least likely "facts" about cats, it at least should be accorded passing reference.

In time the striped wild tabby of North Africa became the striped domestic tabby of Egypt, as the scenario goes, and for a long period its forward movement followed human customs and beliefs more than it did feline biology. The cat became, predictably, an object of veneration and then worship in Egypt. Under no conditions, under threat of death, could anyone kill a cat. People were executed for even killing a cat accidentally. And when a cat died, the whole family, and probably their closest friends, went into mourning, the measure of their personal loss signaled by their shaving off their eyebrows. It was as if a human family member had been poled across to the other side. In fact, that was just how the cat went: mummified and buried in consecrated ground, so many cats that in the last century an enterprising English merchant loaded a ship with their remains and brought them to Manchester, England, to sell as manure. He planned to grind them up, but he found that there was less demand for mummified cats than he had anticipated and ended up with the better part of nineteen tons and very few takers. Eventually he sold them off—dirt cheap, you could say—to anyone who would have them, and fortunately the British Museum and a number of other learned institutions closed in on the hoard and preserved them for their historical value. Today the British Museum is rumored to have a great many mummified cats in its storage rooms. Strange if the "curse of the mummy" is a great big meow.

The names we have for cats today seem to trace back
fairly logically to the language spoken then. Puss or pussy
could easily have been derived from the name of an Egyptian
goddess variously recorded as Pash, Bash, Bast, Bastet and
Bubastis (Bubastis may also have been the name of a town
and a consecrated cat cemetery). If the uncertainty is annoy-
ing, remember that we are dealing with names that have been
mangled by linguists for millennia and that they originally
came into our alphabet from hieroglyphics, probably via
Greek or the high and low Latins of Rome, or Hebrew or
Aramaic or Syriac. The word "tabby" apparently originated
in Turkey, where the word *utabi* is closely associated with the
phenomenon we call the cat. As for the word "cat" itself, in
North Africa there are Berber words very close to that sound
and in Arabic the word *quttah* could have inspired the Romans to *cattus* or *catus*. But it doesn't stop there. In Baghdad
there was a royal line known as the Umayyid who had a special cloth woven for them called *attab*.

Paleolinguists can argue as long as taxonomists, but from
somewhere in that muddle of language, probably between
fifteen hundred and two thousand years before Christ, almost
certainly in Egypt, surely from a wildcat known as *Felis libyca*
or something close to that scientific designation, our domestic
cat arose. It has been straight uphill from there for our part,
and with some high points but also many markedly low ones
for the cats themselves.

One thing seems absolutely certain in all of this: the great
cats of the world never figured in it. As much as we enjoy
seeing the panther in our puss, the lion in our litters, there is
not a shred of evidence that anything like that kind of a mix
ever happened. Yet, wildly exotic mixtures *could* have happened if people had been keen enough to try for them. Today
we list the bobcat as genus *Lynx* and our cat as genus *Felis*,

so by all odds, as members of different genera, not to mention species, those two cats should not be able to breed. Yet one of our fourteen resident cats of the moment is a cross between a bobcat and a domestic tabby.

The reason there aren't more such cases is that crossbreeding is unlikely to occur in the wild—not unknown but unlikely. Cats apparently have at least one sexual scruple, our earlier speculations on *F. chaus* notwithstanding: Don't flirt with he (or she) who might eat you. A big cat would be more likely to kill and perhaps eat a smaller cat than dally with it romantically. Our domestic at-home cats have always despised lions, tigers and cougars, as you will discover if you ever drag your pet cat to a zoo. Presumably they could have found a way, the problems presented by size notwithstanding, but there is little suggestion that they did so.

In fact, cats generally are not the manmade animals most of our other domestic animals are. Such extremely varied canines as the Chihuahua and the bull mastiff, the Dalmatian and the bulldog, all belong to one species. The physical variances of cats have proven to be far less elastic genetically, with nothing like that kind of spread in size or shape—or, for that matter, behavioral purpose. Cats would never permit it. Besides, a house cat the size of a mastiff would make kitchen work impossible—and consider the cost in kitty litter! You would have to mine it yourself and rent a backhoe to do the litter box.

The progress of the domestic cat away from Egypt is almost as hard to trace as are its origins there. The records seem to show that some tame cats (perhaps they were still just tuned down or socialized and had not yet become truly domesticated by selective breeding) were sent as gifts, tribute or trade goods to Palestine, Crete, Greece and Italy. And it seems quite certain that there have been domestic cats in

India for about two thousand years, and elsewhere in Asia for
not quite so long. How did cats get from Egypt to the Malay
peninsula or to China and Japan? It is possible that envoys or
merchants may have taken some cats with them as pets, as
status symbols or as a means of impressing the locals. It is
also probable that cats of marked beauty or specific breeds, as
the breeds began to emerge, may have been carried as trade
goods. Clearly, if you lived in an area where cats were not
known, or barely known, and a merchant showed up with
cages of them, they would command a respectable price.
Who wouldn't want to be the first family on the block with a
silken wonder to display? It is quite likely that merchants who
engaged in trading cats started their journeys with pregnant
cats and bred their offspring along the way. Some journeys
took years—and cats mature to mate in considerably less than
one year. In any case, if we knew more exactly how cats
moved around the world we might know a great deal more
about how and when people did.

In the more northern European latitudes, the confusion
from the first millennium after Christ gets strange. In both
pre-Christian England and Scandinavia we find a legendary
cat sacred to the mother-goddess Freyja. In some stories it
does a very uncatlike thing. It draws Freyja's sled across the
sky. Now everyone knows that reindeer are supposed to do
that kind of work, but there these legendary tabbies were:
draft cats and their godddess.

Whatever motivated the early cat-raising Egyptians to let
some of their sacred charges out of their control, the numbers were almost certainly small. Some of those that did get
packed off to the north, west and east (some may have gone
south, but that area, eastern Africa, is an especially tough
one to follow historically) may then have been crossed with
silvestris in Europe, or with some other subspecies that is

now extinct. Whatever, the cat was still an object of veneration, to be shipped out only sparingly. It wasn't until the
Egyptian religion with its ideas of sanctified animals had been
replaced with Greek and Roman paganism that cats could be
bought and sold as regular commodities, much, in fact, as
they are today.

This was not really a good move for the cat, but the fact
remained that it was Imperial Rome that fostered their spread
throughout Europe. There are remains of cats recorded from
several Roman sites in Britain which suggest that the Romans
not only sent cats around to their friends, but took them with
them wherever they went on their imperial expansions. This
was a long way to carry animals of very little, if any, economic
significance, and with cats having been pretty much phased
out of the god business by the time the Romans reached
Britain, we can reasonably suppose they had become highly
thought of simply as companions.

That may not seem like a remarkable development until
one looks at it more closely. Luxury was no stranger to Egypt
during the dynasties, or to Rome during either the Empire or
the Republic. So it is understandable that cats, being luxury
items, were adored. But as they became more common, and
more commonly owned, the adoration continued. Why? Util-
ity really had nothing to do with it. There were toy dogs by
then in Europe and Asia, and a Shih Tzu is about as economically useful as a tabby cat is. And although mechanical
mousetraps would eventually come along, cats would become
far more popular after the appearance of these competitors
than they were before. Farm cats on patrol in the barn or
around the corncrib are useful, but they are cats at work, not
cats adored. Which brings us to a small anomaly. The more
cats do for us in any practical sense—like ridding a grain bin
of rats and mice—the less likely we are to adore them. Adora-

Cats with a rat, from a medieval bestiary

tion, at least in our relationship to the cat, appears to be connected with its indolence.

The dog, with its powers of adaptation, has a different appeal. Its early ancestors were a social species, and it has been. bred to recognize the dominance of man and to be useful to man. The same can be said of horses, cattle, camels and most of man's other domestic creatures, all of whom have also been good eating, dogs included. (Cats certainly are still eaten in parts of Asia and were sold as meat in Europe,

France particularly, during famines and war blockades, but cats have never been kept as a food animal.)

The early adoration lavished on cats by the Egyptians was a foretaste of much to come. It wasn't the lavish last word, however. Egyptians may have shaved off their eyebrows when puss died, but they probably didn't have cat shows and birthday parties for cats, nor did they publish two dozen cat books every year. Cat cartoons, cat calendars and all the rest of today's cat-oriented paraphernalia were far in the future from the days of King Tut—but seldom has there been a period in history when there weren't signs they were on the way.

So, in the briefest possible form, that is the early history, or at least the background, of the cat. The most important single point to emerge is that man took on the cat because he really wanted it. Even at the beginning he must have detected the potential for a grand affair. Making cats themselves gods and goddesses, or at least companions of deities, was as incidental as all of the nasty business in the man-cat relationship that came between a thousand and fifteen hundred years after Christ. As we will see more fully in a later chapter, it was hell after man turned the cat loose from the bondage of Egyptian adoration. But god or devil, the cat has survived, it has moved on. Ask any cat. It knows where it has been, and it has plenty of places it still intends to go.

Black cat, by Chu Ling,
Chinese, 19th century

3

The Cat
as an Animal

THERE IS a biological reality to the cat that comes before literature, art, religion and lore, the by-products of our own fascination with this creature. The animal has a natural history all its own, and although there are arguments centering on some refined points, the basic cat is now quite well understood, at least from the zoologist's point of view. Behaviorists still have a way to go, for the cat is by nature a keeper of secrets, and quite likely what we don't know about cats is one of the beast's major attractions.

Zoologists place the cats, all of them, in the order CARNIVORA. The term denotes the carnivores or meat eaters, but nothing in natural history is as clear-cut as we would like it to be, so some distinctions have to be made. Not all animals that eat meat are in the order CARNIVORA. The killer whale (really a very large porpoise) eats seals and other whales, but it is not in CARNIVORA. Rats and other rodents will attack young animals in the barn and eat them, but they are not in CARNIVORA either. Chimpanzees and baboons will eat meat, and so will many other animals grouped all over the mammalian family tree. To add just slightly to the confusion, the giant panda is in CARNIVORA, but its diet is at least 95 percent vegetable matter, and both coyotes and foxes will eat berries and melons with relish. Bears are certainly carnivores, but they will pig out on blueberries when they are available and will even graze on grass like cows. What really distinguishes the CARNIVORA are tooth style and structure, and a line of descent from far more ancient mammals.

To be specific, all cats have either twenty-eight or thirty teeth including four "fangs" or canine teeth that serve as stabbing and holding instruments during the kill. They also have a very rough tongue that can strip hair from hide and meat from bones.

What animals, then, are included in the CARNIVORA? Some very diverse mammals and some of the smartest in the world. Among the families included are CANIDAE (the ending -dae in zoology always signifies a family)—the wolves, foxes, jackals and other kin, including our domestic dog. The dogs all shared a comon ancestor with the bears about sixty million years ago, and the bears are included in the CARNIVORA as the family URSIDAE. The family PROCYONIDAE (families, like orders, are shown in full caps) includes the raccoons and their relatives. The weasels (otters, skunks, mink and a good many more) are in the family MUSTELIDAE.

Continuing down the limb of the tree we come upon the family VIVERRIDAE. That group includes the mongooses (it is not mongeese), genets and civets, and a few other even less well known forms—altogether about seventy-five distinct species. (Genets and civets are often referred to as cats, as in "genet cat" and "civet cat." That is wrong, for neither animal is a cat by any twist or turn of the zoological nose. They are viverrines, the CARNIVORA family with the lowest recognition factor.)

Next we encounter the family HYAENIDAE which obviously includes the brown, striped and spotted hyenas, and the aardwolf. Some people have gotten it into their minds that the hyenas are really dogs that were designed by a committee. Actually, they are closer to cats than dogs. In fact the next family *is* FELIDAE, the cat, including our domestic cat. There are thirty-six species of wildcat and one of them essentially gave rise to our house cat as discussed in the preceding chapter.

We could stop here because we have our cat's roots, but there is only a bit left, and we might as well complete the cat's zoological context. The only oddball left, in fact, is the giant panda whose only near relative is the little red panda. Pandas have been called bears (URSIDAE) and raccoons (PROCYONIDAE), but it seems apparent now that they are neither. They need a family all their own. Most zoologists appear to agree, but an argument persists over what to call it. Some say the panda family should be AILURIDAE and others say it should be AILUROPIDAE. It hardly matters in the overall scheme, but as long as zoologists are arguing about that (which they will be doing for a long time) it will keep them out of mischief.

There, then, is our cat, a meat eater whose ancestors trace back perhaps a hundred and fifty million years, when they looked nothing at all like they do now. Back then they were little things scurrying away from giant, often ferocious dinosaurs. But the mammals had the last laugh, and once the dinosaurs packed it in (we still do not really know why that happened) the mammals with their superior brains became the dominant vertebrate forms of life on earth. The insects are far, far older, as are creatures like crocodiles, but the dominant figures on the land remain the mammals as they spread out and became gorillas and giraffes and cats and bears and walruses and all kinds of wonderful creatures.

What distinguishes a mammal? They are generally far more "intelligent" than other animals (compare a bug and a bear, a warbler and a wolf). They also do something the other animals don't do—they produce true milk, which the mother feeds to her young. The glands provided by nature for this task are called mammary glands, hence mammals. Mammals also have hair or fur for at least part of their lives or in at least some quantity, while other animals do not. (The "fur" or "wool" on a furry or woolly-bear caterpillar is neither fur nor wool.) Since birds and mammals both descended from reptiles, feathers and fur are both modifications of scales.

Mammals, at birth, are either precocious or just the opposite. Precocious means that they are able to swing into adultlike action almost at once and may be eating adult food within days or even hours of birth. Hares are precocious, as are guinea pigs. But rabbits (rabbits and hares are closely related and are lagomorphs, not rodents) are not. The babies are pink and helpless, with both their eyes and ears sealed for many days.

Generally speaking, the higher in intelligence an animal is, the slower it is to mature and the more helpless its babies are. Apes are helpless at birth, as are human beings. All cats are that way too and depend on their mother for absolutely everything, especially milk and protection from other predators. Mother cats even protect their babies from disease because the first milk a mammalian mother provides is colos-

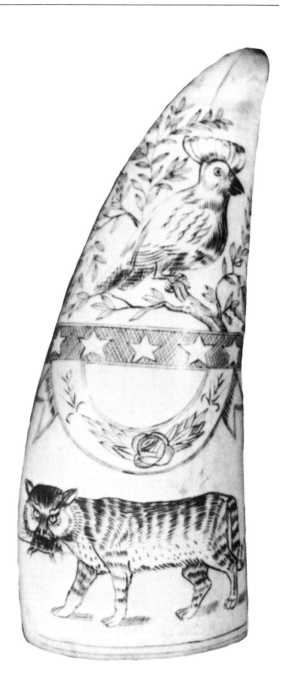

American
scrimshaw carving
of cat with a mouse

trum, which contains antibodies and digestible proteins. Newborn kittens, up to about the age of three days can not digest ordinary proteins. The protein antibodies in the mother's milk for that same length of time protect the kittens against disease. The antibodies pass through the walls of the kitten's gut directly into its bloodstream, and the immunity the mother has built up through her life becomes her baby's protection as well. It is a beautifully designed system, as is everything else about cats.

Barring squealing wheels and brakes or an encounter with a savage dog, a cat's life expectancy is usually given as fourteen years. There have been so many exceptions, however, that the figure is probably low. One famous veterinarian in Connecticut, Dr. Leon Whitney, told my wife that cats can live thirty years if their nutrition is monitored and if they are kept out of harm's way. Certainly many cats live into their twenties. And when the end does come they seem to linger less than other animals, including dogs. When a cat starts downhill there is usually no stopping it. If the cat is an outdoor animal it may just vanish, choosing a quiet, secluded death away from the hollering and whooping back home. Remember, cats are secretive, and it is quite in keeping with their lifelong dignity that they face their end without tears or to-do.

The words pregnancy and gestation are identical in meaning, but we usually reserve the former for human beings. The gestation period of the cat is about sixty-five days, although it can run to seventy or more, and frequently does. Again, as reserved and dignified animals in times of deep purpose and meaning, cats will sneak off and have their kittens in a secluded place if they can. Either that or they will have them on your pillow or on the floor of your closet. It is best to confine a cat as the sixtieth day of gestation comes to pass. A box or basket with a soft lining is a thoughtful gift at such a delicate time, as is a clean dish of water and a well-tended cat box.

There is no one reliable litter size. A silver ash tabby of ours, expected to have a first litter of one or two, delivered nine kittens. A large cat may be expected to have six or seven and deliver one. Cats are perverse in this matter and have as many kittens as they want (figuratively speaking, of course) and cannot be counted on for anything like a fixed number of young.

Cats are perverse in another way. Dogs, much more convenient creatures, go into a twenty-one-day heat or estrus cycle every six months. Cats are maddeningly irregular. They come in and out of heat like shoppers going through swinging doors. There is no planning. Actually, estrus, generally taken to mean the whole reproductive cycle, includes just those days when the cat is receptive to the male, which coincides with the period during which she can actually conceive. Estrus, that catchall term, is divided into four subcycles. Pre-estrus occurs when the follicles on the ovaries are ripening and getting ready to split open and send eggs down to meet, presumably, incoming sperm on the way up. It is then that the female is at her alluring best, when she enters her often noisy courtship stage and sends all the males around her into a tizzy of anticipation, with volunteers up and down the block. Then there is true estrus. The eggs are descending and the female is accepting. Metestrus is the part of the scenario that merges into pregnancy or gestation if sperm and eggs have encountered each other successfully. Anestrus is when the female's sex life goes into a period of quiescence, a blissful time for owners. The period between anestrus and the next pre-estrus may be days, weeks, or months. Only the cat knows and it isn't talking. Owners adopt a wait-and-see attitude.

Lithograph by Edouard Manet

There really isn't anything unusual about the cat's reproductive life. The males do fight among themselves (most mammalian males at least argue with and threaten each other), and the successful male or tom who covers the queen may be very rough. Female cats often get bitten on the back of the neck. They make a great deal of noise about it, but one suspects it isn't all that upsetting in the context in which it occurs, for cats generally are highly motivated in matters pertaining to sex. (It is ironic that a sexually hyperactive human male is called a wolf while his nightly activity or at least his goal is called tomcatting. Zoological metaphors are frequently mixed.)

A cat that is descended from a long line of its own kind is a "purebred" animal as long as it breeds true to others of its kind. Cats that do not reproduce themselves in kind even when bred to their mirror image are not yet purebred. The counterpoint is a cat whose ancestry was rather more casually assembled, and such cats are typically called mongrels or alley cats or by other terms that border on being pejorative. I prefer the term "random-bred" not just because it is an accurate account of what has occurred, but because it has more dignity than "mongrel" or any such descriptive expressions.

Cats, as has been and will be indicated elsewhere, are nowhere near as variable in appearance as dogs are. There are big house cats and small house cats, cats with long, even luxurious, coats and cats with short, or even missing, coats. But there is no spread to equal chow, toy poodle and Irish wolfhound, bloodhound and Pekingese. By dog standards, all cats are not only rather like each other, but not all that different from their North African wildcat ancestry. Even horses range from twenty-one-hand draft horses to Shetland ponies, an eight-fold weight differential. For many people with an undiscerning eye, a cat is a cat and that's that. But, then, some people think all classical music sounds the same and one wine is as good as any other dead grape. To the true connoisseur, cats vary from breed to breed as dramatically as a Van Gogh differs from a Rouault or a Modigliani, a Brancusi from an Epstein. We will treat these variations more fully two chapters hence when we discuss the remarkable range of cat breeds, but for now it's enough to note that to the finely tuned eye cat breeds are individual works of art with their own criteria and are no more alike than fine cheeses are to the palate or Stephen Sondheim and Wagner to the ear. The true cat lover is a person of highly refined tastes and demanding standards. But that is also true of people-loving cats. Discernment is very near the core of the cat/human relationship.

Zoologists pay a great deal of attention to teeth. There are several reasons for this. Teeth are the toughest, longest-lasting part of an animal's body, and when everything else has gone back into the chemistry of the land, teeth are generally still there. Paleontologists have become very sophisticated in attributing specific kinds of teeth to long-dead animals. Teeth are a good gauge for placing animals on their family tree. Cats have the teeth of a hunting/killing meat-eater and are very effective. Typical of most mammals (among mammalian exceptions, elephants get seven sets), cats get two sets of teeth. The first set, or deciduous teeth, appear between the kitten's fourth and sixth week of life. Between the animal's fifteenth and seventeenth week these baby teeth are shed and replaced by teeth that will last the cat for life. By seven months a cat's teeth are all in and fully developed, including those deadly canine or killer teeth. The fact that the four corner teeth in a cat, its longest teeth, are called canines has no significance. They can also be called eyeteeth. Cats don't have wisdom teeth. They don't need them.

Cats use their claws more than almost any other group of mammals. (Sloths and anteaters use theirs as well, but not many other animals do.) All cats have retractable claws, curved nails that can be brought back into sheaths when not in use—all cats, that is, except the rather uncatlike cheetah. The advantage of bringing the claws in when they are not being used to kill, hold, fight or climb is to keep them sharp. The cat has five claws on each foot and they are used in different ways. The front claws are extended when slapping out at something or when holding prey. A cat in real trouble will roll onto its back and rake hard with its hind claws in an effort to disembowl an attacking enemy. All the claws are used in climbing although cats that have been declawed— that is had their front claws removed—can still run up trees amazingly well.

If one listens carefully to the sounds cats make, their voices can be very expressive. Only the great cats have a special larynx that enables them to roar. House cats do not roar although some appear to try (a Siamese cat that could roar would be sociably unacceptable).

Most of the serious cat diseases can now be countered with vaccines. The worst killer of them all, feline leukemia, was known to be caused by a virus for a long time, but only recently has a vaccine become available. Feline infectious peritonitis and feline panleukopenia are two other serious diseases that can now be controlled by medication. Cats with leukemia often developed FAIDS, which means, as you might expect, feline acquired immune deficiency syndrome. The most troublesome ailment is urinary tract blockage. Why a cat's urine becomes gravelly, causing the cat great distress, is not fully understood. It may well be viral and it may have to do with ash content in food. A slightly acidic diet can be helpful—some people add a little tomato juice to their cat's food. Undetected urinary blockage such as might occur in a feral cat must be agonizing before the cat finally succumbs.

Cats' eyes are very sensitive, and although they cannot

see without any light they can operate with far less light than the eyes of a human. Fully open, the pupils are round, but they narrow to vertical slits when the light is bright. Cats are color-blind.

Cats have good hearing, although aging cats may become progressively deaf. In the middle ear there are three small bones known as auditory ossicles, which extend from the eardrum to an opening in the wall of the inner ear, the so-called oval window. In older cats these ossicles change and become less mobile, and when that happens hearing starts to fade. White cats with blue eyes can carry a gene for deafness, and although not all cats with a white coat and blue eyes are deaf, it is always a distinct possiblity. Deaf cats can live very good lives (all cats have a rich internal life) as long as they are protected from things like moving vehicles and snarling dogs. Many people have deaf kittens destroyed as soon as the condition is discovered. That seems like an overreaction. Since most cats don't listen to music or come when they are called except at mealtime, deafness is not the handicap a lot of people make it out to be by way of projection.

On the subject of projection, something must be said about castration and spaying. Very few cats are fine enough examples of their breed to warrant any kind of a sex life. We have such a horrific surplus of kittens every year that it is the absolute duty of the owners of almost all cats to have the males altered (castrated) and the females spayed. People argue that since it is the female that has the kittens there is no need to alter the male's profile. That is specious. A single unaltered male can impregnate scores and scores of females. The best thing that can be said for an unaltered tom is that his owner deserves what he will get. Intact toms wander, fight, run up high veterinary bills, spray urine all around the house to mark territories, and are noisy. They are objectionable animals in most ways and often are far too busy answering impelling calls to duty to become the pets most of us want. Their spraying can make a home all but uninhabitable.

The really remarkable thing about the cat biologically is that while it does descend from an essentially solitary animal, it has become sociable to a high degree. Cats that sit on your lap, rub up against your ankle, rub their cheek against yours (to mark you with pheromones from tiny glands at the corners of their mouths) and sleep on your bed are doing things their ancestors never would do. If you compare the cat's period of domestication, just under four thousand years, with the dog's almost twenty-five thousand years, you will probably come to the same conclusion I have. Cats aren't there yet. They are still very much in transition and will almost certainly be very different in ten thousand years from what they are now.

From the foregoing it should be clear that cats are physically rather average carnivores. They breed, they get born, they get sick, and they get old and then they die. They are agile athletes, they are frequently very pretty, they are skilled hunters, they are elegant and graceful, and, most important of all, they please us marvelously well. We have been together with our cats for a relatively short time. Both cats and their human companions have come a long way, but have a far longer way still to go.

Study by Kuniyoshi

Lady with cat, by Hokusai

4
The Bond

AESTHETICS ASIDE for the moment, along with all of those marvelous literary quotes from the celebrities of pen, brush and quill, there is, as mentioned toward the close of the previous chapter, a remarkable bond of companionship that can come into being between a human being and a cat. Because cats are the least economically significant of man's domestic animals (setting aside aquarium fish, caged birds and land crabs), that bond has to exist or we wouldn't still be keeping them. We probably never would have condoned their leaving the silo patrol unless we had really been keen on exploring broader aesthetic and emotional horizons with them. We did explore, and we declared our findings good. We were correct in our judgment.

What is this bond? It is difficult to define in part because we have really just begun to think about it scientifically. For millennia it has been intuitive and emotional. But let's try. It has many facets, like the cat itself and, for that matter, like ourselves. Together we constitute a blending of the confounding and the confusing.

First, back to aesthetics. Cats are objects of beauty even if they are no longer objects of organized worship. That is simple to demonstrate. Go to any museum, thumb through any art book and what do you find? From ancient Egypt (obviously), from Crete, Peru, France, Germany, Greece, Rome, England, China, Persia, Japan, Java, Italy, the United States, Russia, Spain, Belgium, Holland—from just about all art-producing cultures that have been exposed to the cat, you find a continuum of art masterpieces, or at least important art works of cats as the central or integrated figures. The list of artists may read like a seed catalog, but regard: the Master of Hagia Triada (known to us all, of course), Albrecht Dürer, Hans von Kulmbach, I Yuan-chi from Hunan, Kuniyoshi, Gustave Doré, Pinturicchio, Morris Hirschfield, Paul Davis, Theodore Steinlein, Paul Klee, Francisco de Goya, Foujita, Henri Rousseau, Campagnola, Leonardo da Vinci, Edward Lear, Picasso, Alexander Calder, Gustave Courbet, Marc Chagall, Delacroix, Ingres, Renoir, Andrew Wyeth, Giacometti, George Cruikshank, John Tenniel, Toulouse-Lautrec, Paul Gauguin, Manet, Suzanne Valadon, Watteau, Van Veen, Rembrandt, Bosch, Brueghel the Elder, Honoré Daumier and on, literally for pages. Many of the artists we all know, some only a few of us will recognize by name, but they all had this in common: they could not escape the lure of the cat. Nor could uncounted and unnamed masters of altar carvings, illuminated manuscripts, friezes and virtually every other technique and expressive medium known to man. There is no trouble proving that the most acute eyes, the

Drawing by John Singer Sargent

most sensitive souls have turned to the cat for inspiration, allegory and the sheer joy of capturing a magnificent form in repose or motion. Anyone who would deny that cats are beautiful will have to run counter to every school of art we know, and most all of their greatest practitioners. Cats are things of beauty, and there is enough pure celebrity attached to that premise to make contrary argument relatively uninspiring. After all, who would want to argue with Ingres, Picasso, Watteau or the Master of Hagia Triada?

So we have, in the cat, living art. But what is its appeal beyond beauty? To a large degree the cat is a mystery—and mysteries are as attractive to most people as is beauty. The cat is knowledge beyond our own, it is an insight into life that is different from and therefore seemingly as profound as ours, possibly more profound than ours. Cats are, as we suggested, hedonistic materialists, and so are human beings (except those who make a career out of selflessness). We share this very important characteristic with the cat and admire the beast for that reason. A cat knows how to be comfortable, how to get the people around it to serve it. In a tranquil domestic situation, the cat is a veritable manipulative genius. It seeks the soft, it seeks the warm, it prefers the quiet and it loves to be full. It displays, when it gets its own way in these matters, a degree of contentment we would all like to emulate. If we could relax like a cat we would probably live at least a hundred and twenty-five years, and then we could relax to death. Cats know how not to get ulcers. We may seek that level of tranquility, but we seldom achieve it. In our homes, with us paying the bills and knocking our heads against the wall trying to keep it all together, the cat does cool out as if by birthright. And, of course, it does so by birthright. Although far too many millions of cats are born because of their libido rather than our planning, it can be said that the domestic cat is here because of us.

So we have beauty and we have tranquil role models as the begining of the explanation of the bond, for the cat's beauty is no less a source of wonder than its skill in hedonistic pursuits. There is more.

Strangely, because nothing in the cat's background or origins would suggest that such a thing was possible, cats interact with us in a very direct way. Cats make one of the most satisfying sounds in the world: they purr. I have never heard an explanation for the purr that I felt comfortable with, but I certainly feel comfortable with the phenomenon itself. Almost all cats make us feel good about ourselves because they let us know they feel good about us, about themselves, and about our relationship with them. A purring cat is a form of high praise, like a gold star on a test paper. It is reinforcement of something we would all like to believe about ourselves—that we are nice. After all, since we create such nice conditions for a "dumb animal" (though one we are never quite sure isn't really wiser than we are), we must be nice. Somehow, in our apparently selfless way (which is wishful thinking), we have created a setting that our litmus test, the cat, has tried out for us and with us, and the cat's purr tells us we have succeeded. I think a lot of us wish we could purr, and in that spontaneous verbal (yet nonverbal) way tell each other how much we approve. Purring people would have to feel good about themselves and each other. Imagine how you would feel if you bumped into someone in an elevator and they purred instead of glared at you. And instead of muttering a self-conscious "Excuse me" you could purr back.

Still, cats are not quite as up front about satisfaction as dogs are. If a dog is pleased with a set of conditions he wants you to know right then and there. He licks your hand. He wipes the coffee table clean of bric-a-brac with his eternally wagging tail. He hops and flops and flounces and pounces and displays in every way possible to tell you how grand a master you are and how successful you have been at putting good things together. Cats just look at you through half-closed eyes and purr and purr and purr. We like that, in fact most of us like it both ways, and that is why more and more homes are harboring both species. The silly bromide "fighting like cats and dogs" is another of those attitudes or beliefs that are based on lack of real experience. There are certainly cat-killing dogs, and cats that will never forgive a dog for its canine heritage, but generally speaking cats and dogs are more accepting of each other than cats are of cats or, very often, dogs of dogs. Puppies and kittens raised together are eternally friendly. Dogs often learn a lot from cats about demeanor and self-respect. (If cats learn anything from dogs, they generally keep it to themselves.)

When cats interact with us directly, their size is a comfortable one for us to manage. Cats rub their cheeks against our ankles and, if we pick them up on cue, against our chin. (We may want to believe this is out of pure affection, but they also do it to mark us as their property.) They cuddle, they roll into a ball and sleep on our laps. Cats' fur provides, in virtually all breeds, a pleasing, tranquilizing tactile experience. No worry stone ever felt as good (and besides, worry stones can't purr).

The way a cat arches its back and moves its hips sideways to encounter our caress is a further approbation. We are doing it right. Cats, when we make them feel good, make us feel good. It is all part of the cat's technique, and it works. You can go all day through the *sturm und drang* of professional and social accomplishment and never feel as downright good as when your cat tells you that he or she approves of you. Cats give us quite willingly what our fellow humans are all too often loath to give us. Many people, when they give you well-deserved *Attaboys*, act as if they were giving up something they really needed to hang on to. Cats give us all

Woodblock print by Hiroshige

the *Attaboys* we want and never diminish themselves. In the philosophy of the cat, if it could be expressed, we would find, "It doesn't cost anything to be nice." Cats are not only very well mannered, they are also magnanimous. They seem to comprehend our needs and, like benevolent monarchs (if cats could talk they would surely use the royal We), give gentle gestures of approval.

An amazing aspect of all this is that we are reasonably sure cats understand none of it. When we stop being anthropomorphic, stop assigning human traits to distinctly nonhuman cats, we are forced to concede that cats probably operate at an intelligence level about the same as that of the dog and the pig. Now in the scheme of animal life that is high, very high, but it is far too low to actually comprehend the things we have been talking about. Experience these things, yes; understand them, no. Still, it is fun when you pat your cat to pretend.

It is all the more remarkable, then, how it all works for the cat. The cat has evolved to give the appearance of wisdom and to act as if it interacted with us in a way designed by it to make us feel good about ourselves. We may pretend there is more to it, but in truth it is simply the nature of the cat displaying itself. We were destined by that nature to be interlocked with cats almost as soon as we discovered their potential for at least some genetic manipulation and their natural love of the hearth.

One thing I will give cats in all of this—they do love. No one can tell me cats do not in some way feel something for us that transcends the full stomach and the warm cushion. Those are what they demand, not what they feel about us. On their own level, in their own way, and certainly by their own choice, my cats think the world of me. I don't know if gratitude is involved, and I don't know if some vestigial or perhaps nascent social sense is at play, but cats seek my company, like my lap, want to be on the foot of my bed even when there are lots of other soft places around. We have a thing going, and it has been viewed by both the cats and me as good. To me, that amounts to love.

Another thing about the cat that attracts us and keeps us in there supplying all the good things in life is that very part of the cat that eludes us. Cats have retained enough of their wild heritage to fascinate us. They are a window into the world on the other side of the wall, where the jungle begins. Once upon a time we were hunters and worked the woods and fields for whatever they had to offer with no prior input from us of agriculture and husbandry. Cats never went through that developmental phase. They were taken in as hunters and given what they needed—everything, that is, except the evidently ineradicable need for the hunt as a thing unto itself. That is why cats (and unfortunately a lot of people we call sportsmen) are still recreational killers.

As our kittens grow we see them stalk their own tail, or the tail of anything else in the room. We see them pounce on a dust-fluff ball or a rug tassel or on our own feet. From almost the very start, once they are walking, they start training for the hunting sessions they need never experience unless they want to. Strangely, they all seem to want to. You can make virtually any cat flatten its ears, scrunch down and go cross-eyed by slowly dragging a strip of cloth across the floor. If a mouse should pop out of the bread drawer you will see virtually every cat in view electrified, even if they have just been fed. Most cats never lose their wild side. And when one appears to do so, it can be rare enough to make the papers. I have always loved this snippet from a British newspaper—I don't know which one, or its date, except that Victoria was queen:

SAGACITY OF A CAT

. . . a story is given as well as vouched for, of a cat that
had been brought up in amity with a bird; and being one
day observed to seize suddenly hold of the latter, which
happened to be perched out of its cage, on examining, it
was found that a stray cat had entered the room and that
this alarming step was a manoeuvre to save the bird till
the intruder should depart.

There is fascination when the cat plays his role, stalks
and hunts, pounces and, yes, kills. All of us who have cats
that go out into the yard have found offerings. Chipmunks
are found on the doorstep, sad little reminders of what we
have taken into our lives. Mice, moles and shrews appear as
if by magic on our pillows, even garter snakes on the living-
room couch. Such offerings testify not only to the fact that
our cats are still able to catch their own food, should they
ever need to, but that they seem to want either to remind us
of that fact or to please us with small gifts most of us would
rather do without. And, strangely, our fascination with the
cat's retained killer skills is, as the story of the sagacious cat
gives evidence, equaled by our fascination with the fact that
some cats manage to overcome what comes naturally and
accept mice as companions or even birds as friends. No matter what the cat does, it fascinates us. I am not sure whether
this is because cats are so like us or because they are so very
different. It could be either, or both.

There is another far-reaching aspect of the man-cat
bond. We may not understand it, but at least we are beginning to wonder about it. There is a growing body of evidence,
as I guess you could call it, still far more statistical than em-
pirical, that suggests cats are beneficial to our health, even
our longevity.

At the School of Veterinary Medicine at the University

of Pennsylvania there is an innovative effort called The Center for the Interaction of Animals and Society. At The Humane Society of the United States in Washington, D.C., there is the Institute for the Study of Animal Problems. At the University of Washington in Pullman there is the Delta Society. These groups and many more just appearing are trying to put together both the historical perspective and the present realities of man and animal as a team, with the cat included as much as any other beast. Science has now decided that there is something important in such team relationships.

From the studies and findings of these groups, it now seems certain that the tactile sensation of cat fur we spoke of is actually a tranquilizer. It also seems certain that even seeing a cat in repose provides us with a genuine role model to which we react as we would to another person's yawn. Ease is catching, repose is infectious, peace can be epidemic. The cat is a carrier of them all. It has been said often enough by now (but it is worth repeating in the context of house-cat companionship) that people who have pets, who have managed to bond to even a nonhuman companion, tend to live longer than people who have not been able to achieve such a relationship.

Although no one is suggesting that they are a panacea (a placebo would be more likely), cats may not only give their owners longer lives but healthier ones. Bonded people tend to get sick less often than nonbonded people, and when they do get sick they seem to get milder forms of their ailments. Patting a cat lowers blood pressure—this has been demonstrated again and again.

No one is really certain what gland or organ is involved, but scientists are looking into it. If it is true that pets create a healthier, longer-lived ambience—and I, for one, am sure it

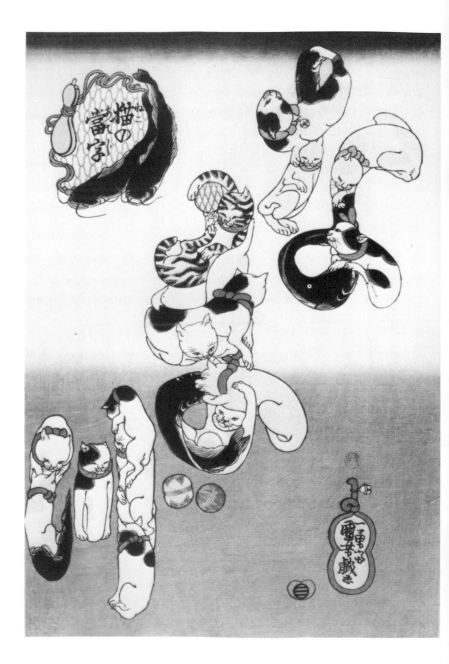

Cats forming the Japanese word for "catfish,"
by Kuniyoshi

is—this means that while we were selectively breeding cats to be what we wanted them to be, they were, in a very real sense, selectively breeding us to be cat lovers. After all, if a cat has someone on the hook who is providing the good things in life, it is to the cat's advantage to keep that person going not only to produce offspring with the same characteristics but to infect any offspring already on the ground, or perhaps even friends, with a highly desirable trait from the cat's point of view. Put simply, it is in the interest of the cat to perpetuate what is good for the cat.

And so the cat may have forced us to inadvertently manipulate our own genes in favor of its well-being. The idea appeals to me as an amusing, delightful irony. Thank heavens, though, that they don't have us spayed and altered, as we do them. There is no telling what standards they would adopt.

Studies for the fifty-three stages of the Tokaido,
by Kuniyoshi

5

The Breeds

WE KNOW cats today in a far greater variety than our ancestors did. Thanks to those battalions of cat designers known as breeders, we can at least reasonably predict what a litter of purebred cats will look like. That's *purebred*—the term "thoroughbred" does not apply to cats any more than it does to dogs. A *thoroughbred* is a specific breed of horse. If there were such a thing as a thoroughbred cat, or dog, it would be a very strange animal and I am not sure we would know what to do with it.

The breeding of cats is strictly for pure breeds. When we let our cats wander, not having had them altered or spayed, almost anything can be there when the litter appears. It is a terrible thing to allow unwanted cats to be born. Millions have to be put to death every year for want of homes. It is the greatest sin against cats we can commit.

When we do breed purebred cats, what may we get? By no means do all cat fanciers or all cat organizations agree on the appropriate breed standards, and there is even controversy on which designations are actual breeds and which are not. We can, however, go with a fairly reliable consensus that there are about eleven breeds of longhair domestic cats and twenty breeds or thereabouts of shorthair cats. In each of these categories there are endless varieties usually based on color, some of which are considered breeds unto themselves.

Very often their names, designating one country or another, have nothing to do with their geographical origin. The acknowledged exceptions are usually stated as the Siamese, which came from Thailand (formerly Siam), maybe (although most authorities agree that the Siamese bobtail probably originated in Japan), and the Manx, which came from the Isle of Man, perhaps. In fact, though, there are numerous exceptions, we think. The Maine Coon cat did occur in Maine as well as along the seaboard of the other New England States, but the Russian blue is probably quite a bit more Scandinavian than Russian, and the Havana brown was developed in England, not Cuba. The Bombay does not trace back to India but to the Burmese cat, which does not trace back to Burma, and to the American shorthair, which traces back to everywhere. It is all a big muddle, and it is best to let the name stand for the cat, not for a place on the map.

The most popular of all purebred shorthairs is, hands down, the Siamese. More of these are registered than any other pure breed. The Siamese has "points," or areas, of intense color, and it is the color of these points that identifies the kind of Siamese you are dealing with. The face, most of the head, the ears, legs and tail constitute the points. The basic body color of very light coffee with lots of cream may be washed, particularly along the spine and on the shoulders and thigh, with some hint of the point color. All Siamese are born creamy white all over, and the points and washing come along later as the kitten matures.

The most popular Siamese variety is the seal point. That was the original Siamese, and to many people it is still the only one. It is as if these fanciers want to deny all of the grand things breeders have done over the decades to broaden the Siamese horizon. The blue point came after the seal and is probably the second best-known color, having supposedly come to England from Thailand at the end of the last century; the earliest record of one being seen is at a show in London, the Holland House Cat Show, in 1896. Then, there are the chocolate-point, lilac-point, red-point and tortie-point Siamese. (There are no tortie-point males, just as there are no tortoiseshell or "calico" males outside the ranks of Siamese. The gene for tortoiseshellness is carried only by females.) And there is a Siamese that was known in Scotland back in the 1940s as the silver point, and is today variously known as a tabby point, lynx point or color-point shorthair. Then there is a whole array of other Siamese configurations best referred to as "all other." If that isn't good enough for you, you may find yourself enmeshed with cream point, red and cream tabby points, and tortoiseshell-tabby points, which can be seal, chocolate cream or lilac. One of the cat registries, The International Cat Association (TICA), is proposing yet another Siamese breed to be called, provisionally, the snowshoe. This is a Siamese seal-point cat with additional white markings. Specimens can be spectacularly beautiful, and probably this will be considered a breed of its own before too much longer.

Today's Siamese is much finer boned, much more slender, with a smaller, more pointed head and face than the

Siamese I knew forty years ago as a kid. It is a super-refined beast with an enormous personality. Certainly Siamese are among the most lovable and devoted of pets. They never stop talking, and they insist on being involved in everything that is going on around them. Usually they get along well with other cats and with dogs. They have loud, insistent voices, and when I grew up it was generally believed that in their native Thailand they were used as watchcats. They certainly can be noisy enough to have filled that role. Females that have not been spayed are just plain awful when in heat, and the males can be almost as bad; the Siamese libido is a thing of wonder, both awesome and loud. Most people who switch from the joy of the random-bred cat (which we knew in Boston way back then as "Chauncy alley cats") usually go first to the Siamese. There are more of them, and they are the breed the uninitiated are most likely to associate with the first rung of the feline social ladder. (And no two ways about it, that ladder exists.)

Other shorthair breeds fall into British and American categories. Among the general types known in England are the bicoloured, black, blue-cream, British blue (including a variety known as the Chartreuse), cream, spotted, brown tabby, red tabby, silver tabby, tortoiseshell, tortoiseshell and white, and white. The Cat Fanciers Association in the United States lists the following as American-type shorthairs: white, black, blue, red, cream, chinchilla, shaded silver, red chinchilla or shell cameo, red shaded or shaded cameo, black smoke, blue smoke, red or cameo smoke, classic tabby, mackerel tabby, patched tabby, brown-patched tabby, blue-patched tabby, silver-patched tabby, silver tabby, red tabby, brown tabby, blue tabby, cream tabby, cameo tabby, tortoiseshell, calico, dilute calico, blue-cream and bicolor. It has come to a point where a lot of people at cat shows, including a few judges, don't know what they are looking at unless they

From The Histoire of Four-Footed Beastes, 1658

can see a sign on the cage. There are so many gradations, mutations, secret crosses and other variables as to leave one utterly bewildered, certainly far more so than is likely in the dog world. It is, after all, much easier to tell a Great Dane from a St. Bernard than it is to tell a calico from a dilute calico (even if the Great Dane came from Germany and not Denmark). But, then, what's in a name? Precious little.

As if to make it absolutely certain that no one can start catching up in the arcane world of purebred cats, there are now what are referred to as Oriental shorthair types. We will skip over them, just as we will skip over the American wire-haired cats. They figure somewhere between the long- and shorthair breeds, presumably, and may be spontaneous mutations with many if not all of the same colors as the shorthairs. But I don't think the breeders in their secret meetings need fear our ever catching up with them. No sooner do we nonprofessionals think we may be about to understand what is going on than it is announced that a rare new litter has appeared on a farm near Tucson and the breeders, cat designers, and namers are off loping down the road ahead of us. Let's leave it simply with the fact that in America there are also "exotic" shorthairs in just about the same variety of colors and patterns as there are in England and mainland Europe. To state it in the easiest terms possible, the exotic American shorthair, in most of the colors previously described, has a broader face and somewhat less of a neck than the "regular" American shorthair.

The endlessly amusing Abyssinian—whether ruddy, red or blue (all three are recognized)—is supposed to have come to us from Abyssinia, but that is highly unlikely. A Mrs. Barrett Lennard is said to have come home from Abyssinia in the 1880s with at least one example of the breed, but it is far more likely that the animal was evolved in Europe and America from very selective breeding, the way almost all of our other breeds were. Abyssinians are long, lean and extremely athletic cats whose behavior is quite off the wall. They stalk visitors as if they were escaped gerbils, charge, tumble, jump up on the nearest promising lap, snuggle and then go off the wall again. They play at being spooky, but they really aren't if they have been well socialized. In short, the Aby is a fun animal to have around, with enough class to challenge any Siamese. Although it tends to be a little goofier than the Siamese, it is seldom as noisy. The Abyssinian is not a casual cat, either in price or in the social demands it makes.

The Burmese is another popular shorthair breed that would seem to put the lie to the statement that the Siamese and Manx are the only geographically accurate cat names. They say that the Burmese did come from Burma, showing up in San Francisco in the 1930s. Perhaps and perhaps not. Burmese clearly have a lot of Siamese in them, and whether the mixing in of Siamese blood was done here or whether the original so-called Burmese was a solidly colored Siamese is very difficult to say. The Burmese is a nightmare to judge at shows because the difference between any two Burmese is likely to be extremely subtle. Mature Burmese are usually a rich and very warm sable all over, with the slightest shading toward a lighter hue underneath. They are luxurious, aristocratic cats of great beauty and style. Some fanciers claim blue and chocolate-and-frost varieties, and probably these colors will be recognized as distinct breeds at some future date. The Burmese is just starting what should be a stunning career in America.

One strange characteristic of these three exquisite "non-American" luxury cats is that they do tend to be class conscious. There are exceptions, of course (as there always are when dealing with cats), but if you have a mixed household of cats the Siamese will tend to seek out other Siamese and hang out together, probably gossiping about the low station of the un-Siamese cats, just as Burmese will seek out Burmese and Abyssinians other Abys. I don't know how they know, but they do. Fortunately these socially prominent breeds do let people into their tight little circles, and I guess we should be thankful for that.

A *19th-century Russian cat*

The Russian blue, as indicated earlier, may be another cat that came from the place its name suggests, as well as from parts of Scandinavia. They are mind-bogglingly beautiful animals—clear blue in color without any markings—and should have, ideally, vivid green, almond-shaped eyes. With their fairly long, tapering tail and graceful build, they are a cat to behold. Relatively few of them exist, and five or six hundred dollars would be about right for an average kitten. This is a serious, heavy-duty cat best for someone who has already had Siamese, and perhaps another breed or two. Russian blues are active, very alert cats and seek endless interaction with their human family. They get along better with other cats than do most exotic breeds, and their curiosity is boundless.

Earlier in this chapter we mentioned the Havana brown. These cats are mahogany-colored, without markings, and have eyes that range from green to chartreuse. They are another of the super-pretty cats, and probably there have never been any in Cuba. They were actually developed in England, where they were first called "chestnut foreign brown." They are expensive and just plain works of art—truly a cat fancier's cat.

We mentioned the Oriental shorthairs as recognized in the United States. These come in all of the expected colors and should have long, slender, tapering heads, although lately some breeders have been producing so-called Oriental shorthairs that look more and more like American pinheads. Let's hope that in time the trend reverses. These very finely bred cats, characteristically long-legged and slender, should become more popular. Right now they are special cats for special cat people.

The Egyptian Mau may really have come to England from Egypt, and is said to be the only naturally spotted cat we know. Maus come in three colors: light silver with charcoal markings, honey-colored bronze with dark brown markings, and a luminous black ground color called smoke, with charcoal spots. Their distinctly almond-shaped eyes should be gooseberry green, often with a slight amber cast to them. The effect of that cast in any of the three colors is head-turning. To confuse the breed standards somewhat, the British now have a cat known as the Oriental spotted tabby, presumably the cat they once called the Egyptian Mau, but this cat was bred to be spotted, unlike the naturally spotted Mau. The eyes run copper to green depending on the body's ground color. If this seems confusing, one suspects it is supposed to be.

The lovable silver-blue Korat, like the Siamese, is believed by many cat fanciers to have originated in Thailand, though it is said to be rare even in that part of the world. It certainly is here. The matter of origin, once again, is speculative. It has large, luminous eyes that seem always to be on you, penetrating, analyzing, containing all the mysteries of the East. Korats are not easily available, as breeders tend to be possessive and want to know where their treasures are going. I say more power to them. Luxury should not be peddled to impulse buyers like so many truck-garden crops at roadside stands.

American breeders began experimenting with crosses between the black American shorthair and the Burmese a few years ago and came up with a breed known today as the Bombay. This all-black cat with gold to deep copper eyes is not only new—it is rare to the point where many cat fanciers would not know one if they were holding it. The wonderful sheen of the Bombay's coat is its giveaway, as is its most pleasant disposition.

In 1950 a litter of kittens was born in Cornwall, England, to a perfectly normal tortoiseshell-and-white cat owned by a Mrs. Ennismore. She noticed that something was unusual, if not wrong, with a male kitten named Kallibunker. The cat had a distinctly curly coat. He was mated back to his mother, and several curly-coated kittens appeared. When Kallibunker finally died, one of his sons, Poldhu, continued the trait, and we now have a breed called the Rex. It is a strange animal.

Not only do Rexes have curly coats, but their body temperature is higher than that of other cats, and they are far more athletic than their common ancestors. Following the British example, after some hesitation, we in America recognized the Cornish Rex and the Devon Rex as two different breeds. The strange characteristics of the Rex are said to be natural mutations, and both strains are now bred around the world. Rexes are fascinating cats, and although not exactly what you will find being given away from a cardboard box in a supermarket parking lot, they are attracting a great deal of attention. They come in a wide range of normal shorthair colors, and recently the Cornish Rex has done itself one better: it has thrown virtually hairless cats (the ears alone have almost normal fur) that are called, for no reason at all, Sphynx. They are considerably warmer than normal cats, to compensate for their nakedness, more so even than the standard Rexes. They are still very rare. Another natural mutation and nobody knows where it will end. Indeed it may end where it is, for the Sphynx seems to be a mule. The male I met had been bred three times with no offspring yet in sight.

The Scottish fold is another apparently natural mutation, one that in fact did appear first in Scotland. It has ears that are folded over just about one hundred and eighty degrees more than normal, giving the strangely appealing cat a rounder face than can be found in any other breed. The allowable colors run the gamut of both American and British (and exotic Oriental) shorthairs. Scottish folds are hardly common, but like the Rex and the Sphynx they do have an appeal that is all their own. Just how much of a role earlier such mutations had in the evolution of our puss-by-the-fire can not be reckoned. It seems certain that features like the folded ears and the curly coat could not have been bred for without spontaneous mutation. It is interesting that while dogs show tremendous genetic flexibility that responds to our tastes, cats, lacking that flexibility, throw natural mutations of their own choosing. But then, cats are more stubborn than dogs in many ways. It shouldn't surprise us that even their genes like to play by their own rules.

The origin of the Manx cat is nicely contradictory. On the one hand the breed is said to be one of the few that come from where they are supposed to have come from—the Manx, from the Isle of Man. But even the Manx may be geographically misnamed. One popular story has it that tailless Middle Eastern cats were picked up by a sea captain who, in 1558, got lured into the Spanish Armada fiasco; his ship went on the rocks, on the Spanish Rock to be precise, hard by the Isle of Man. Some of the tailless cats made it to shore, and that is how the strange cat with the strange tail and a rabbitlike gait got where we found it. Whatever the truth, the Isle of Man has some cats with either no tail, some tail, or pretty nearly a normal tail. It is, then, not true that Manx cats are necessarily or altogether tailless. They do hop like rabbits, though, making them one of the most interesting shorthair cats around today. They are not really rare—just expensive. They come in most of the usual colors and combinations of colors.

The Japanese bobtail does indeed come from Japan, where it is known and has been for centuries, as Mi-ke. It is often tricolored—black, red and white—and as its American name suggests, has a tail between two and three inches long. It is very appealing as a kitten (but, then, what cat isn't?), and it grows up to be a cat of above-average intelligence. Or putting it less anthropomorphically, it grows up to be a cat willing to display and use whatever intelligence it has—which, to the owner, is pretty much the same thing. It should be pointed out that there is a whole array of other colors possible for this breed, and all are allowed.

For a long time it was thought that the Somali—which most definitely does not come from Somalia—was another of those spontaneous mutations which probably have done so much to alter the history of the domestic cat. The mutation this time was conjectured to have occurred among Abyssinians. The somewhat longer coat of this still shorthaired cat was bred for in England around the turn of the century, using Abyssinians and a British longhaired breed. Here again, we may never know—but we do have this elegant cat, ruddy, with gold or green eyes, or red with the same eye-color range. Somalis are delightful pets and there aren't enough of them around to keep up with the demand. This is a cat for a dedicated cat person or art lover. It will add grace and charm and rich, lustrous warmth of color to any environment.

One thing about cats—there are always plenty of new breeds waiting in the wings for recognition. In addition to these shorthair cats recognized by the CFA (Cat Fanciers Association), there are others recognized by TICA (The International Cat Association). The Tonkinese (also spelled Tonkanese) is a cross between the Burmese and the Siamese. TICA wants to give it breed status, CFA still says no because it doesn't produce predictable young. Time will decide on the Tonkinese, as it will on the Singapura, which is said to have come here from Singapore in 1975 and is also championed by TICA. Still another case of TICA saying *oui* and CFA saying *non* is the Chartreux, a breed said to have been known in France as far back as 1723, although it didn't get to our shores, as far as we can be sure, until 1970.

If we have nailed down the origin of the domestic cat in general to *Felis libyca*, we are far less certain about the longhaired cats in our homes today. It has been pretty well ruled out, as we mentioned in an earlier chapter, that the European wildcat or *manul* cat added the longhaired gene. It is more likely that it was a characteristic that could be bred for, either because there was a mutation in that direction or because the cat's genes were flexible enough to let it happen when man became insistent. Hiding in short-coated to moderately coated cats was a long coat. We found it and bred for it. This all seems to have begun with a chap named Pietro della Valle, of obviously Italianate persuasion, who lived from 1586 to 1652. Pietro was obsessed with travel, and toward the end of his life he brought some longhaired domestic cats to Italy, probably from Asia or Asia Minor. There do not seem to be records of the transactions involved, or at least they haven't been discovered yet. Later in the seventeenth century, a French gentleman and scientist got some of these cats in Italy and took them north into France. By the time they reached Great Britain they were being called the French cat. The French naturalist and prolific writer Buffon called them Angora cats in an uncharacteristic moment of counterchauvinism, Angora being the name of the Turkish city we now call Ankara. It was thus established, with very little information to support the premise, that longhaired cats came from Turkey, where they had been developed by selective breeding or had emerged as a natural mutation.

By the middle of the eighteenth century the British, having taken the glory away from the French and even the Turks, began calling the longhaired cats, which were still attracting an enormous amount of attention, Persians. For decades, even centuries after that, Angoras, which may have come, but by no means certainly came, from Turkey, and the Persian, which may never have seen what is today called Iran, were interbred. It was genetic folly that was bound to fade because they are really distinctly different cats. The Persian we know today, compared with the Angora, has a much more distinctly pushed-in face—a description not meant to be pejorative, for they are exquisite animals.

Painting of a cat by Goshun,
Japanese, 18th century

Today's Persian longhair, about as pretty as a cat can be, comes in an amazing array of colors: white and black, obviously, but also blue, red-self (solid color), cream, chinchilla, pewter, shaded silver, chocolate, chinchilla golden, shaded golden, red chinchilla (also known as shell cameo), shaded cameo (red shaded), shell tortoiseshell, shaded tortoiseshell, black smoke, blue smoke, red smoke or cameo red, smoke tortoiseshell, classic tabby, mackerel tabby, patched tabby, brown patched tabby, blue patched tabby, silver patched tabby, silver tabby, red tabby, brown tabby, blue tabby, cream tabby, cameo tabby, tortoiseshell, calico, dilute calico, blue-cream bicolor, Persian Van bicolor, lilac, Peke-face red and Peke-face red tabby. If a fancier can't find his or her own Persian in that lot he or she should give up and raise rabbits or guinea pigs instead. Just to keep the complexities complex, in the white Persian alone there is a blue-eyed variety, an orange-eyed variety, and one known as the odd-eyed, which calls for one eye to be blue and the other either orange or copper.

Persians are delightful companion animals, but they do need help with their coats. A Persian can work up a hairball you can take bowling. They need to be brushed, and their snags have to be worked out without jerking the poor creatures into splotched bald patterns. These are definitely not cats you let out to play in the rose garden or beyond. It doesn't take long for their crowning glory (actually, in large part, their owner's achievement) to become a walking nightmare. Many Persians hate to be combed out, but this is one argument the owner simply has to settle in his own favor.

Several times before this century, breeders tried without notable success to cross longhaired Persians (usually whites) with Siamese to get a truly longhaired Siamese. Then, for a brief time in the 1920s, a cat called the Malayan Persian was bred in the United States, but specimens were either not very hardy or not very fertile. They disappeared. Finally, sometime after World War II a blue Persian was crossed with a Siamese to make the dream come true. For no reason whatsoever the cat was called the Himalayan, even though it is really a luxuriantly coated Siamese. Himalayans are also referred to as colorpoints; they can have about as many different point colors as conventional Siamese, even though they look like Persians, with their shortened faces and the glory of that coat. They are delightful as kittens and outstanding as companion animals when they mature. They also get along well with other animals and, despite the nonsense of their name, they are one of the world's great cats.

Nothing about cats can remain simple, however, and the Siamese offshoot story does not end there. In the 1950s some cats appeared that had the Siamese patterns but distinctly fluffy hair. In time they came to be called Balinese, again for no good reason except that so many of the other romantic place names had been used up. They, too, are longish-haired cats with the Siamese pattern. Why are they not Himalayans? Because they do not have the Persian face. Balinese are longish-haired Siamese that are far more Siamese than Persian in look, style and temperament; Himalayans are longhaired Siamese that look and act like Persians. We are simply going to have to live with it.

There is a third cat of this general design. Called the Birman, it is the sacred cat of Burma. All kinds of legends go with this presumed denizen of the temples. It is longhaired and does have a vaguely Siamese look, except that the paws are white and the dark markings on the face don't reach all the way to the ears. Birmans are seen in a number of color phases, as are the Siamese and Himalayans, but they are, on sight, a different cat and one of incredible beauty. They are very expensive, and very few are around. Birmans are splendid, powerfully built creatures, though not as lithe as the Siamese we know in America and Great Britain.

In 1955 two travelers in Turkey, reportedly in the vicinity of Lake Van, found some Turkish Angoras that probably were fairly close to the Angoras that preceded the Persians in western Europe a few centuries earlier. So suddenly we had the old Angora back, first in pure chalky white, later to be bred into other colors and patterns. We now have them in black, blue and smoke. They are distinctly longhaired cats, but do not have anything like the characteristic Persian shortened face. I have owned only one of this breed. Unfortunately, as so often happens with white longhairs, he has been deaf from birth. He is also clearly retarded, unable to learn very much from experience, but we are certain he has a rich internal life. My son says he is the only cat that can sit for two and a half hours and watch the wall go by.

In the 1850s, they say, seamen brought some longhaired cats to Maine and ports just south that were bred with very hardy local shorthaired stock and produced the Maine Coon cat. It is pure rubbish that the mix contains any raccoon. Cats are miraculous animals, to be sure, but not that miraculous. Crocodile would be as likely a mix, or giant squid.

The large and robust Maine Coon cat comes in a variety of colors and makes a remarkable pet. The large, wide-set and slightly oblique eyes of these cats can be shades of green, gold or copper (white Coon cats have blue or odd eyes) and are ever watchful, ever questioning, ever seeking an opportunity to interact. These are affectionate cats just about large and tough enough to pull sleds.

A few other odd varieties round out the list. In the United States there is a longhaired Manx that is called the Cymric, and another longhaired variety that TICA calls the Ragdoll and the CFA does not acknowledge. No doubt, in the years ahead, new breeds will emerge and be given all manner of romantic names. Cat fanciers have no limit when it comes to imagination. The one universal failing they appear to have is geographical determination. Thank heavens the Vikings, Phoenicians, Portuguese, Spanish, French, Italian and British navigators did not use cat fanciers to create their charts and record their voyages, or we might have a cat called the Congo that originated somewhere between the Nile and Yangtze Rivers.

Study by Kuniyoshi

Cat by Robert Leydenfrost

6
The Cat Show

THE FIRST THING you have to accept about cat shows is that they are not anything like horse shows or dog shows. They are closer to rabbit shows, canary shows and guinea pig shows. At a horse show, even though there are confirmation classes—that is, competition based on how well a horse is put together—there is still action involving people. There are usually riders on those horses, so performance is a very large factor. No one rides a cat over a fence or a fakey brick wall at a cat show.

Most dog shows are confirmation shows, also based on how well a dog is put together according to its breed's standards. There are obedience trials and other specialty field events, but the term "dog show" most often refers to the judging of a dog's skeleton (which the judge can't really see, but can guess at), also its coat, feet, pasterns, tail, testicles and other assorted parts.

At any dog show, even a confirmation show, there is, again, performance on the part of the dog in partnership with a handler. The handler may or may not be the owner as well. The dog is required to move at a fixed speed through a few prescribed maneuvers so the judge can evaluate its skeleton and musculature. The animal has to be "set up," put into a standing position so the judge can evaluate the animal's topline, length of neck, tail set, ear set and other angles and areas against the standard recognized for that breed. A good handler is one who can set up or "stack" a dog in a way to hide its faults and thereby fool the judge.

In contrast, at a cat show all the performances are given by the owners and occasionally by a particularly flamboyant judge. The cats don't do a thing except resent the indignity. They are brought to the arena looking cross and put upon, are placed in numbered cages, and sit there with all kinds of funny signs hung on their individual cages. Typical of these signs are, I ♡ MY CAT; I DON'T BITE, MY MUMMY DOES: NO FINGERS PLEASE; KITTENS FOR SALE. The cage usually has a bed, a tiny bowl of water and a small litter box requiring the cat to make its toilet in front of crowds of people, something I feel certain the cats resent. Cats are naturally private animals, and if you watch a cat in its box at a show it seems to overcome the public indignity of the experience by going slightly cross-eyed and looking as if it had just signed the Declaration of Independence.

A loudspeaker goes nonstop at cat shows, summoning cats to their respective rings and telling people they are double-parked. When a breed and number are called, the owner or handler grabs the cat from its cage and rushes like O. J. Simpson to the proper ring, where the cat is popped into another smaller cage. If it is a longhaired cat and has been dusted with powder, it is not unusual for it to be carried upside down by all four legs and shaken as it is moved through the crowd (making it advisable not to wear dark blue or black to cat shows).

There is an unwritten rule for spectators at cat shows: Don't touch. Cats are extremely susceptible to respiratory diseases, and most such ailments are highly contagious, via humans no less than other cats. Touching cats at cat shows can pass ailments along, and this is unfair to the cats and the people who have invested heavily in them and, more importantly, love them. Show cats are generally very good sports and will tolerate prodding to a remarkable degree, but it isn't nice and you shouldn't do it. Leave the poking to the judges. They know how.

You can sit ringside and watch the judging, which can be instructive. It is a good way to learn about styles and standards, and it certainly provides an opportunity to see some breathtaking animals. You will note that the judge wipes his or her hands with a medicated cloth before touching a cat, and that the table where the cat is placed for examination is also wiped down with a medicated substance before each contestant is put in place. Cat shows are very clean events, as suits the nature of the beast.

The most surprising thing a judge does is to raise the cat into the air and stretch it out as if he were contemplating a pelt for a coat, perish the thought. This cat-show stretch is *de rigueur*, and the cats apparently get used to it. Perhaps it even feels good after sitting in cramped cages and carriers for hours on end. The judge will examine the cat's outer coat and its undercoat, if there is one. He will examine the eyes for color and clarity, length of tail, set of ears, and he will try to peek at the cat's teeth. I have seen a lot of judges give up on that part of it when the cat flashed a "go ahead, make my day" look.

Cat washing, by Hiroshige

Generally, except for a certain loss of dignity, cats are not hurt or harmed by going to cat shows, unless someone has brought an unhealthy animal into the show arena. But all cats at shows are certain to be up on their shots.

One big difference between dog and cat shows is that dogs don't really stand a chance at a show unless they love the hustle and the fuss—a dog that slinks around like a salamander under a low-hanging rock just won't catch the judges' imagination—whereas cats are not really expected to get into the spirit of things. I know that not everyone will agree with me, and certainly different cats act differently, but I don't think cats ever really like shows. Clearly attitude has a lot less to do with winning for cats than is true among dogs. Cats can be awfully good sports about human nonsense, and I think most of them just give up and go along with the whole show scene. They do get a lot of extra attention and are often fed from tiny jars of baby food, which cats adore. And the experience does give them a chance to look even more indignant than usual. (We assume they would want to if they could.)

The purpose of cat shows, ostensibly, is the same as that of dog shows. Setting aside human ego (a big factor in any animal show, though one never acknowledged officially), the plan is to select those examples of a breed that are best suited to carry forward the genetic potential of that breed. There are standards, and those cats that come closest to perfection and get most of the great big multicolored rosetted ribbons and ugly trophies get the most bids to breed. And their owners get the highest prices for their kittens. So, although I doubt that a tomcat ever makes the connection, seen from a male perspective, the more ribbons a tomcat wins the more action he gets later. It can get to be fun for the cat at that point, and potentially big business for the owner. But, "big" is a relative term here. The truth is that most cat breeders who care about their cats lose money on every litter.

I have been to many cat shows as a spectator, but my wife and I have actually shown only one cat, and her only once. She is a silver ash tabby exotic shorthair named Maridadi. Mari won four ribbons at her one show and fortunately didn't get any respiratory ailments. I caught a terrible cold, however, and (not that it was the reason) we haven't shown a cat since. Somehow Maridadi got one of her ribbons into her cage and chewed up and swallowed half of it, so she ended up with three and a half ribbons and some colorful stools. Still, not a bad take for one day.

The first cat beauty contest in the United States is generally believed to have occurred in New York City in 1895. A more organized event took place in Chicago in 1899, and that is considered the cat fancy's first significant splash. (The word "fancy" comes from the Olde English and means "to bet." Which leaves one rather puzzled. People usually don't bet at cat shows, at least not that I am aware of. I can't imagine calling a bookie and saying, "Give me ten bucks on the blue-eyed silver Angora in ring nine to win.") Today most cat shows are either all-breed shows or specialty shows. Usually, specialty shows are limited to either longhaired breeds or shorthaired breeds.

There are several cat-show organizations in the United States, and their rules vary. If you are interested in showing your cat and you have had it properly registered, you can write to the secretary of your local cat club, which sponsors one or more shows a year, and get an entry form. Send in your fee, show up at the cat show with your bowls, brushes, combs, food, litter, signs, trays, photographs and sensible shoes and try to look as if you weren't terrified or confused—not that many others there will know what they are doing, either. Those few who do will be easy to spot. They will have people standing around them desperately trying to hear every word they are saying. The people are generally nice enough, and since your cat, who is even more confused than you are, is playing the game with a stiff upper whisker, you should do no less. They don't punish people who make mistakes or miss a breed call, so don't panic. Let it happen.

Most cat shows of any importance will be held between September and February. That is when coated cats will be wearing their finest; queens are frequently littering in the spring and summer months in between. Toms can be difficult to handle in that warmer time, too, so not too much is likely to happen after March 1.

You will be checked out by a veterinarian when you enter the hall, or, more accurately, your cat will be checked out. You will go to your designated cage and get yourself and your cat comfortable. For yourself, a camp chair is a must— your feet will soon enough be killing you. A thermos bottle presumably full of hot coffee can be helpful. (For some reason, bourbon neat and whiskey sours are popular at cat shows.) Get to know the people at the next cage. You may end up friends for life.

The Cat Fanciers Association, Inc. (CFA) is the heavy-duty group in this country when it comes to cats, and here are a few of their rules. Kittens qualify as such at a cat show only up to the age of eight months. Spayed or neutered kittens may not be shown. Unlike dog shows, where "dogs" are male and "bitches" are female (they are never called Dog & Bitch Shows, however), all cats, as long as they are over eight months old—male, female, spayed, neutered—are called, unsurprisingly, cats. There are three major categories for competition: Non-Championship, Championship and Premiereship. The latter group is for altered cats (not kittens, remember). Within each of these three categories there are various competitive classes. The Non-Championship classes include Kitten, AOV (Any Other Variety, covering registered cats that for some reason don't quite conform to their breed standard—they can win in their class, get a nice ribbon, but cannot become champions), Provisional Breed (cats of breeds not yet officially recognized; again, a cat can only get an award in its own class and cannot yet soar into the rarefied strata of championship competition), Miscellaneous (really a noncompetitive group), and Household Pet (cats that can't become Champions but can win ribbons).

Championship classes include Novice (cats that have not yet won a winner's ribbon), Open (cats not yet Champions), Champion (where the Champions clash), and Grand Champion (the big hitters, who generally lead the most exciting sex lives).

The Premiere classes, as indicated, are for spayed or neutered cats. Since they are not going to be rewarded with a rich social life because of the ribbons they win, we assume they get special treats to eat. They are shown as Novice, Open, Premiere, and Grand Premiere competitors, with the same distinctions that apply to those classes in the championship category.

There are a number of other breakdowns by color and variety that may or may not be used at all shows. The Cat Fanciers Association requires, or at least requests, a Best and Second Best for each category. Other associations want Best and Best Opposite Sex (opposite from the one that wins Best, of course) in all the various divisions and colors.

Now, what is a Champion? This gets tricky, but don't panic. You can always come back later and refresh your memory. Ready? A Champion is a cat that—pause—has taken six or more winner's ribbons designating it as the best cat at that show of its sex in a specific color division for its breed in combined Novice and Open competitions under a minimum of four different judges. It is all there—if you read it enough times you will have it. A Grand Champion, or Grand Premiereship cat, must have accumulated one hundred and fifty points under a minimum of three different judges. It gets points by walking across the bodies of lesser cats—that is, one point is awarded for every Champion the cat defeats in its breed or division. It is much simpler than it sounds.

There are all kinds of other champion formats. The International Cat Association (TICA) has an Aggregate Best of the Best at some of its shows. The cats don't get points for winning that title, but it is a major happening in the life of the owner and breeder (or lives, if they are different people). In addition, the TICA rules call for the judge to select the top ten cats in the show within each major category—kittens for example. Most of the clubs and registries and cat-show organizations print simply worded booklets that explain their way of doing things. They are written for third-graders, so almost anyone can follow along.

I am sure there are millions of cat owners who don't even know there are such things as cat shows, but, in a way, that is their loss. A cat show is a thing unto itself. It serves its own ends, along with the purposes of those relatively few people for whom cats are a business: people who don't just "have some cats" but operate catteries where unaltered males can spray to their hearts content and females can yowl up a storm discussing with each other things we could never understand about feline libido.

I don't think people who show their cats, or who make cat clubs and shows a significant part of their lives, love their cats any more or less than anyone else. They do it sometimes out of natural human competitiveness, sometimes for the action. Cat shows are social events; on rare occasions they are a business investment. The only thing certain is that the cats couldn't care less. The letter that follows here shows just how much of an event it can be. Note the last four paragraphs. Cats have, if nothing else, taught us how to enjoy ourselves.

February 22, 1985

Mr. Roger Caras
ABC NEWS
7 West 66th Street
New York, New York 10023

Dear Mr. Caras:

On April 1, the nation's most outstanding feline will be presented the most prestigious honor a four-footed pure-bred can receive—The Fancy Feast Cup. The Waterford, cut-crystal cup honors only the creme de la creme of catdom, or that feline that displays the patrician characteristics most clearly approximating a breed's perfections as determined by the standards set forth by the Cat Fancier's Association.

Strutting before a panel of tuxedoed judges will be hundreds of fancy felines—representing 26 breeds (from the tailless Manx to the luxurious Persian) at the annual Empire Cat Show, Saturday and Sunday, March 30–31. The Empire Cat Show is sponsored by the Empire Cat Club—one of the oldest cat clubs in the United States, and the oldest of the 500 Cat Fanciers' Association clubs.

Preliminary judging for the cup will take place throughout the show, culminating Sunday night, when the show's top cats vie for the coveted Fancy Feast Cup —the grand finale of the show.

Although the winners and runners-up will be determined Sunday evening, the winner will be officially awarded the cup during the gala Fancy Feast champagne reception in the gilded drawing room of the Helmsley Palace Hotel, located at 455 Madison Avenue, on April 1.

All top feline contestants and their owners will enter the drawing room via a red carpeted staircase. Once assembled, Richard Gebhardt, president of the Empire Cat Club, and fellow judges, will recreate the Fancy Feast Cup competition—hoisting felines into the air to judge muscle tone and disposition.

The judges will then announce—as in the Miss America beauty pageant—the runners-up by presenting them with individual rosettes. Once announced, the winner will be ensconced in a place of honor—a crown-topped chair—where he or she will be serenaded by strolling violinists playing medleys from the Broadway show "Cats" and other feline favorites.

Guests will dine beneath grand chandeliers and elaborate frescoes on brunch fare served by waiters in tuxedos.

We invite you to join us in raising a glass of champagne in honor of these exquisite Championship Class cats—each in a class by itself.

1821 Wilshire Boulevard, Suite 400   Santa Monica, California 90403 (213)829-1840

Cat in Tall Grass,
by Carl Walters

Ra, the sun god, as a yellow cat, killing the serpent Apophis, god of darkness and chaos, Egyptian

7

Mythology
and Core

CLEARLY, a creature as miraculous in appearance as the cat couldn't pass though our lives without attracting a good deal of arcane attention. We have mentioned that the Egyptians worshiped and mummified cats and that the Norse folk had them acting like reindeer in the sky with a goddess in tow— but there is much more. Cats have been at the center of some incredible beliefs, and have often suffered as a result. None of this has been the cat's fault.

No one knows when the cat was first sanctified in Egypt, and as far as the records so far uncovered show, it was never *officially* listed as a god. It was, however, perceived as one—at the least, that is, as an animal sacred to the gods—a perception that went on for at least two thousand years. There are carvings, papyri, statues and engravings that show priests kneeling before bejeweled cats, clearly praying and making offerings. Whether the cat was an avenue to the gods in every case or whether some cults actually prayed to the cat itself is not clear. There are other pictures from the dynastic period showing cats receiving gifts of food and flowers at altars that were clearly their own. King Shishak, referred to in the Old Testament, who ransacked Jerusalem and carried off the Hebrews into slavery, is known to have worshiped the cat. One suspects the line between divine and sacred, god and friends of the gods, frequently got thin in ancient Egypt, and not until new texts and papyri are found will we be able to define exactly what the cat was and what it was supposedly able to do.

The Egyptian goddess Isis was believed to have held the cat sacred. In fact, cats were often considered incarnations of Isis. When Isis's daughter married the sun-god Osiris she gave birth to the catheaded goddess Bastet or Bast, also Basht or Pasht. There were lionheaded goddesses, too, Tefnut and Sekhmet, and their provinces overlapped with Bast's domain. A cat was revered as the mother of the sun-god Nefertem (he may not have been a 100 percent god, but he was well up there) and of the moon-god Ptah.

During the last thousand years or so of Egyptian paganism, Bastet, the catheaded goddess, was frequently either confused with or blended with the two lionheaded goddesses, attesting to the Egyptians' majesterial view of their cats' personalities. East of the Nile delta was the temple complex and city of Bubastis. It was there that the cat cult centered at least three thousand years ago and where so many mummified cats were buried in sanctified ground (and later became a drug on the Manchester fertilizer market). Bastet, the catheaded goddess, was known as a Lady of the East or Lady of Ankh-taui. Sekhmet, one of the lionheaded goddesses, was called the

Lady of the West and ruled on the other side of the Nile. Centuries later the two were blended, confused, and often said to be one creature instead of two. All of this occurred well before Rome, Cleopatra, and the collapse of Egypt's majesty.

Eventually, King Osorkon II built a huge hall in Bubastis dedicated to Bastet. The king endowed the catheaded goddess with enormous power, and wall reliefs were carved to commemorate both the event and the animal. It was probably as high as the cat has ever risen in human affairs. Herodotus described the temple complex in 450 B.C, and apparently it was a wonder of the ancient world. A great many cats lived in the temples, tended by maidens and priests, and were incorporated in all forms of sacred doings. In April and May boatloads of flute- and cymbal-playing men and women made a pilgrimage up the Nile to Bubastis to celebrate the festival of the catheaded goddess. It has been described as a rather bawdy affair with a great deal of drinking and erotic exhibitionism.

There are cat amulets, cat jewelry and statuary of all kinds to mark this period when cat adoration reached levels of ecstasy that would never occur again. It went on for centuries and involved millions of people. Interestingly enough, satirical papyri of the time show cats battling rats, so even the bawdy, ecstatic Egyptians at the height of their cat worship did not lose sight of what had interested them in the wildcats they found patrolling their silos many centuries before. In fact, in all of man's time with cats, despite all of the mysterious, hysterical and blatantly mad events that ensued, the cat has not forgotten how to rat, and man has not forgotten that that was what the cat was originally all about.

Cats have always loved the sun and have been associated with it in the minds of many people from very diverse cultures. There are still Chinese who believe the size of a cat's pupils designates the height of the sun, and that they can tell the time by lifting a cat's eyelid and examining the pupil. I can't imagine that the cats enjoy being thus used as clocks, but their association with the sun does go far back. Although in the Egyptians' complex pantheon the power of the sun was a male factor, Bastet was an exception. Wearing a cat's head, she was, at least for a time, worshiped as a form of the sun and the source of all light.

The Egyptians, in fact, had trouble with darkness. According to them, when the sun went over the edge of the world at dusk, a cosmic battle ensued between Apep the serpent of darkness and Ra the god of light. In later legends of which we have good records, Ra referred to himself as the Great Cat. When a solar eclipse occurred, the Egyptians ran around shaking rattles to waken the cat in the heavens to destroy the serpent Apep and give the sun back to them.

In our own time we play, as did many primitive peoples, a string game known as "cat's cradle." In all likelihood the purpose of the game was to trace the sun's movements and ensnare the cosmic cat who could keep evil forces, anything from Apep to the Devil, from gobbling up the sun and denying man the light he needs to live—that is, the sun that nourishes his crops. Eventually the Egyptians worked out a sacred trilogy, Sekhmet-Bast-Ra. It gets a bit confusing because although Sekhmet was one of the goddesses with the head of a lion, Bast could give up her cat head and wear a lion's head as well.

One of the sacred scarabs was in the form of a cat, and another carried a cat on its back. At Heliopolis, the statue of the deity was a cat. The cat moved back and forth through the religions of the Egyptians like a leitmotif, never far from the center of things both sacred and profane.

It wasn't only the sun that marked the cat's sacred qualities. Ancient Greeks recorded that when the world began the
sun created the lion and the moon the cat. The Greek Phal-
arius was so taken by the cat-moon connection that he
claimed the cat's body grew and diminished according to the
phases of the moon. Plutarch, with no more logic than Phal-
arius, said that cats bore first one kitten, then two, then three,
until the litter reached twenty-eight, corresponding to the
twenty-eight degrees of the light of the moon. Then, not at
all surprisingly, the cat stopped having kittens. Litters of kittens were to Plutarch what the speed of light is to us—a final
measure. Since it is certain that Plutarch never saw a litter of
kittens that even approached twenty-eight, why would he say
such a thing? It is difficult to say at this distance, but perhaps
it was allegorical, or perhaps he did believe it.

On the Isle of Man, at a place called Kirk Braddan, there
is a runic cross built into a wall that is clearly a relic of moon-
cat worship. There are three cats and one shrew in the design.
It has been interpreted that the animals represented the
phases of the moon.

The Greeks believed that their gods were chased into
Egypt by a terrible monster named Typhon, which surely has
something to do with our name for a great sea storm. One of
the goddesses, Artemis, changed herself into a cat and hid in
the moon. The Egyptians saw the cat as a moon-goddess no
less than a sun-goddess, according to the Greeks.

From the very beginning cats have also been associated
with eternity. When a cat curls up it forms a circle, a circle is
endless, and so, it has so often been believed, is the cat—as
is a snake; indeed, in this context cats and snakes have always
been viewed interchangeably.

It is no small coincidence that cats are said to have nine
lives. At various times there has appeared to be nothing but

The cat-witch of Okabe, by Kuniyoshi

reason for such an absurd belief. Nine is a trinity of trinities, and trinities have been focal points in many more religions than Christianity. The River Styx encompassed the Greeks' version of hell nine times, and the Teutonic myths have Odin giving Freyja the power over nine worlds. Egyptian astronomy involved nine spheres, and Apollo, so said the Greeks, created the lunar year consisting of nine months. The time of Christ's death was the ninth hour. The fact that in mythology cats have nine lives shows how close cats have remained to the center of man's universe. On the other hand, typical of the eternal contradictions surrounding the animal, the mummified cats of the Egyptians proved that they were held to be immortal.

On Africa's Gold Coast (Ghana), there are tribes that still believe that a person passes into the body of a cat at the moment of death. In Japan, it was believed by certain sects that a black patch on the back of a cat was a sacred mark and designated that therein dwelt the soul of an ancestor. Such cats used to be sent to special temples for particular care. With their enormously well-developed sense of aesthetics, the Japanese, surely one of the most sophisticated people in the world, have revered the cat and represented it in their art as beautifully as any culture ever has. They have treated it like a flower.

There are lovely myths about Siamese cats. Shadowy patches on the Siamese's neck are thumbprints of the gods left when a god picked up a cat to admire it. In times past, when a monarch died in Siam, and perhaps even lesser members of royalty as well, a Siamese cat was buried alive with the body—but not to die. Holes large enough for the cat to escape through were provided, and when the cat, bored with the tomb, came squiggling out, it meant the deceased's soul had escaped to heaven. The cat, recaptured, was carried off to a special temple with great honors. As late as 1926, when a young king was crowned in Siam, a white cat was carried in the procession in a gilded cage resting on the most ornate of cushions. Things are no less ornate in Burma, where cats still participate in elaborate rituals in underground temples.

So, what started in Egypt still goes on today in some

corner of the world. How much was simultaneous or subsequent invention, how much of it came by way of trading ships and caravans, cannot be determined. But of one thing we can be sure: a great deal of lore, many gods and goddesses, much religion and love of beauty, have ridden the world over on the back of the cat. Almost from the beginning in Egypt the cat has been a vector of culture. The Egyptian word *mau*, as noted earlier, is used to designate a modern breed. It is the ancient Egyptian name for cat, and while its etymological origin is not difficult to imagine, *mau* also means "to see." Indeed, the cat has been associated with sight and foresight and all manner of mystic perception. The Jewish Talmud states that the placenta of the first litter of a black cat who in turn belonged to her mother's first litter should be burned and made into a powder and rubbed into the eyes. This, it was said, would give the person the power to see demons. Long ago in England, the mere presence of a tortoiseshell cat could impart clairvoyant powers to the beholders, and such cats were much sought after as playmates for children. In old France, peasants believed that a black cat turned loose at a juncture of five roads would lead one immediately to buried treasure—a belief unlikely to have tested out as well as some others.

The battle the old Egyptian cats had with the serpent Apep every night and on the occasions of every solar eclipse is not hard to understand. As vermin-killers, cats were expected to deal with cobras, which they often did very effectively, largely because cats are intelligent mammals and cobras are particularly dumb, even for snakes. In Paraguay today cats are used for hunting rattlesnakes, which is far more impressive than dealing with cobras because rattlesnakes are both faster and smarter than their hooded Asian counterparts.

In Japan, the ailments cats are supposed to cure include stomach spasms, melancholia and epilepsy. Black cats serve best, apparently. In a number of places cat fur has been used to treat both burns and rheumatism. It is reported that the Dutch once believed that the skin of a newly killed cat was good for inflammations. Cat skin has been used to treat everything from sore throats to hives. Troubled people in Scotland were thought to be cured of their delusions and wild fantasies by cats. In the Middle Ages, reminiscent of the aforementioned Talmudic belief, the head of a black cat burned and turned to a powder was supposed to be blown into the eyes of a blind person three times a day until sight returned. One has the feeling that being black was not always the best choice for cats.

Sometimes the cat didn't have to die to help people in distress. In Northamptonshire, England, a single hair plucked from the tip of a black cat's tail on the first night of a full moon could be used to cure a sty or a swollen eyelid. You drew the hair across the lid—you guessed it, nine times—and the ailment would vanish. One supposes the cats weren't pleased with having their tails plucked, but it had to be better than having their heads chopped off or their skins peeled away.

The Indo-European word *ghad* was the root from which the Greek, Latin, Russian, Arabic, German and French words for cat arose. *Ghad* means to grasp or catch. In the Talmud the word for cat translates as "the pouncer." Again, clearly, however else the cat reckoned in people's lives, the fact that it was an adept hunter was never lost, never far away. A Russian fable has a cat and a dog guarding the entrance to Paradise. The Devil tries to sneak past, gets by the dog, but the cat, a superior hunter, makes the catch. Aesop told the sad fable of a young man who fell in love with a cat. He prayed to Venus to transform his true love into a more appropriate form, and she responded. As the young man and his bride lay in their wedding embrace the girl looked up, saw a mouse, and took off after it. Venus, realizing that not even her decisions were all perfect, changed the girl back into a cat.

As if the legend of Noah and his Ark weren't difficult enough to handle zoologically, there is a legend on top of that legend and, sure enough, it involves the cat. There were no cats when Noah built the Ark, the story goes, but true to his pledge if not his good sense, Noah took mice and rats on board. They reproduced like the rodents they are, and soon the Ark was overrun with vermin. Noah asked the lion for help. The great beast sneezed, and out of his nostrils blew the world's first domestic cats to clear up the rodent problem with dispatch.

The Italians have a lovely legend. St. Francis, alone in his cell, tried to devote himself to prayer without distraction. The Devil, determined to interrupt the holy man's flow of supplication, sent hundreds of mice to bullyrag him. They nibbled on his toes and almost drove him mad. The distraction was so great that he was about to interrupt his prayers when a cat jumped out of his sleeve and hit the mice like a cyclone. Only two of the whole lot escaped by hiding in a crack in the wall. To this day, goes the legend, cats sit in front of holes in the wall waiting for those last two tormentors of St. Francis to appear.

An eclipse has always been difficult for primitive people to handle, and more than one royal astronomer went to his death for failing to predict one. Cats have long been associated with eclipses one way or another. Some American Indian tribes see a waning moon as something being eaten away by mice. A cat can clear that problem up, obviously, and does

The cat goddess Bastet sailing down the Nile in a barge, Egyptian

so regularly. In West Africa some tribes say a lunar eclipse occurs when a cat eats the moon. They use a peculiar slow hand-clapping ritual to convince the solar cat to release the moon.

Drought has always been one of the most difficult conditions for agricultural people to deal with. The more primitive the agriculture the harder the times when rains fail. In the Celebes, rain was induced by tying a cat in a sedan chair, carrying it around the parched fields, dousing it with water and calling for rain as the cat mewed in protest. In Malaya cats were brought close to death by drowning in a plea to the gods for rain. A black cat was used in Sumatra to bring the rain by tossing it into a river and forcing it to swim ashore pursued by yowling women. In England to this day cats are thought to foretell rain by the way they bathe themselves, or if they sneeze. In the Chinese *Book of Rites*, a cat-god named Li Shou is designated as the recipient of an exuberant harvest festival. Sacrifices, in this case, were made to the cat, who was credited with protecting the crops against rats and mice. This would seem to go back to Egypt, where Osiris was accorded the same respect and honor for the same reasons.

The propinquity and power of the tomcat was regarded highly by the Mochica of northern Peru. Much of their pottery is erotic, and one theme often repeated was the image of the god Ai Apaec, a wrinkled old man-cat god whose domain included medicine and copulation. A Scottish belief, rather difficult to trace to any logical procedure, says that if a tomcat ejaculates while jumping over food, any woman eating that food will give birth to kittens. In 1654 a case was tried in Scotland involving a woman seeking an abortion because she claimed to have kittens in her womb. Remember, we are speaking of a time over fifty years after the death of Queen Elizabeth I, when yacht racing and the greenhouse culture of pineapples had come to the British Isles. We are not speaking of ancient times.

The unhappy truth is that cats have had to take the dreadful with the glorious from beliefs and superstition through much of western history. Mankind has gone as far in one direction as the other, and rarely to more cruel extremes than in the annals of Roman Catholicism. In Vosges, France, cats were traditionally burned alive on Shrove Tuesday. What that had to do with Christ or Christianity has never been clear, except perhaps by that time cats were perceived as agents of evil, familiars of witches and companions of the Devil. The same attitudes were to be found in Alsace, where cats were immolated every Easter Sunday. In the Ardennes, the burning occurred on the first Sunday in Lent. But it wasn't just in the countryside where such atrocities took place. In Paris, on the Place de Grève, baskets, barrels and sacks of cats were heaped high and set afire as part of a Midsummer's celebration. In 1648, Louis XIV himself lit the fire and danced around the pyre as heaven alone knows how many cats screamed in agony.

Oddly enough, the cat has never been officially identified as evil in Roman Catholicism. Between the ninth and the nineteenth century thousands of animals ranging from moles, locusts and serpents to pigs, dolphins and horseflies were excommunicated by the Catholic Church for various sins against humanity (many of them rather more economic than spiritual), but there is not a single cat on the lists I have seen. Eels in 1225, a sow in 1386 in Falaise, a horse in 1389 in Dijon, an ox in 1405, rats and bloodsuckers in 1451 in Berne, but not one cat. The last known case of animal proscription was a dog in Delemont in Switzerland in 1906. Why cats were never excommunicated is difficult to understand. It can't be because the Church did not feel it had the power to do this, since everything from wolves to locusts was so dealt with. Was it because the Church did not want to take on an animal that had so often and for so long been deemed sacred? We can only speculate, because it is doubtful that Church historians even want to talk about that nonsense now.

Folklore has been described rather grandly as ". . . the debris of exploded mythologies adrift on the stream of popular tradition." Such folklore has given rise to some extraordinarily grotesque theology, anathematization and excommunication of animals being the least of it. Even more bizarre has been the capital punishment of animals. Pigs and bulls and dogs have been dressed as humans and brought before the bar of justice to stand trial for biting or goring or killing someone, then marched to the gallows and hanged. This has happened uncounted hundreds of times, yet, again, never does one find a cat in such a situation. It is strange, at least, that while cats were ritually burned by the thousands to celebrate Christian occasions, they were never called before the secular bar or chucked out by the Church.

Until fairly recent times, Europe in general had an appalling record in its treatment of animals. In 1772 a handbill was passed out in Vienna announcing eleven big events to be performed by Imperial License in the Great Amphitheater. The first event called for "a wild Hungarian Ox . . ." with fire under his tail and firecrackers fastened to his ears, horns and other parts of his body to be set upon by dogs. The eleventh event had a "furious and hungry bear" which had been starved for eight days attack a young wild bull and eat him alive on the spot. A wolf was to be held in reserve to help the bear in case he wasn't up to it. Cats did not escape such meets. In 1777 a shepherd at Beverly, Yorkshire, ate a large black tomcat alive on fair day. And on March 1, 1788, the fifth Duke of Bedford—credited earlier in the *Sporting Mag-*

azine as "a gentle man with all the nicer sensibilities of the heart . . . those amiable qualities that so highly honour human nature"—this same Duke put up four hundred pounds against Lord Barrymore's five hundred pounds that Barrymore couldn't produce a man who would eat a cat alive. A laboring man of Harpenden, near St. Albans, won his Lordship his bet. Apparently the standards of the day for "sensibilities of the heart" were not too stringent.

It is interesting but horrifying to note that today, in America, pit-bull owners who fight their dogs in clandestine pits train them by trapping cats or falsely claiming them from shelters and pounds only to dangle them alive from ropes over training pits, forcing their dogs to jump higher and higher in order to tear the cats' heads off.

Back, though, to Europe, and the cat's association with witchcraft. In 1484, Pope Innocent VIII, a gentleman misnamed for sure, decreed that in the future when witches went to the stake their cats were to be burned along with them. As late as the sixteen-hundreds, simply owning a cat could be enough proof to condemn a woman as a witch. Cats connected with witchcraft—on something less than certain proof, one suspects—were dipped in boiling oil, burned, thrown from towers on holidays and beaten to death with whips, scourges and knotted ropes. There are records of cats being crucified, scalded and flayed alive.

How can we explain the cat's association with witches and witchcraft? Before there was anything at all in the cosmos there was a goddess named Diana. She was the goddess of darkness and eventually divided herself into two—she retained darkness for herself and turned light over to the brother she had created from herself, Lucifer. She then desired her brother, but he would have none of it, apparently seeing it as the ultimate exercise in incest. But Lucifer had a magical cat that slept by his side, and Diana somehow got to the cat and convinced it to change places with her. From this position of advantage, Diana managed to get herself with child and gave birth to Aradia. Diana packed her child off to teach people about witchcraft, which she did with great success. Black magic came into being at that point, in the name of Diana, Queen of the Witches, and cats have never been far from the phenomena of witchcraft and magic ever since.

There is another association of the cat almost diametrically opposed to witchcraft that fed into Christianity. It didn't take the domesticators of the cat long to determine that their new charges were highly sexed, and thus the cat became a symbol of motherhood. Bastet and Isis in Egypt, Demeter in Greece and the Celtic Cerridwen were all earth-goddesses who gave birth to the spirit of maize and were pictured in the form of a cat. Yet there was a profoundly illogical side to our old friend Bastet as a goddess of fecundity, love, maternity and the birthing room. Like the Greek cat-goddess Artemis, Bastet was worshiped as a virgin! And when Christianity rolled upward into Europe collapsing whole systems of beliefs, Bastet, Isis, Demeter, Cerridwen—all who had eventually taken the form of cats—surrendered to Mary as the divine Virgin Mother. Legends said that at the moment of Christ's birth in the manger a cat under the floor of the manger gave birth to kittens. That allegory has appeared again and again in paintings by Baroccio, Leonardo da Vinci and other masters who depicted the Holy Family. A cat is very often in view. In the thirteenth century, cats were the only animals permitted to dwell with the sisters in English nunneries.

The cat has had benevolent associations, both religious and secular, for traits other than the maternal. In Chinese Buddhism the cat is the symbol of self-possession. The

Roman goddess of liberty has a cat by her feet. Roman legions often used cats on their banners as they set forth to terrorize the world. An alpine troop of legionnaires had a cat with one eye and one ear (the symbolism of which appears to have been lost). The Swiss used the cat as a symbol of liberty, the Dutch used the cat as their ensign. St. Yves, the patron saint of lawyers, is often portrayed with a cat by his side.

Yet while all of this was familiar to the people of the times and in the places referred to, the cat was still being burned and impaled and crucified and flayed, either for superstitions related to witchcraft or for other associations with evil derived from some ancient belief.

The Germans had a goddess named Hel, and the Greeks had Hecate, both represented by black cats, and both omens of death. Tales continue to this day of black phantom cats warning of the approach of death, or of people dying after seeing such a cat. The silly belief that a black cat who crosses one's path will bring bad luck is alive and well in America today. People deny of course, that they believe it, but still would rather not have it happen. The Chinese believe the black cat is the harbinger of sickness and poverty and the French and Germans have parallel beliefs. Nonsense knows no geography, and neither do domestic cats, for wherever there has been cat religion, lore, abuse or adoration, it is absolutely certain there have been cats.

We know that cats were objects of trade and were carried as symbols of status and exotica. Did the legends that so often parallel them, thousands of miles apart, travel with them? Did the magical aura of Egyptian, then Grecian and Roman gods and goddesses, travel as adjuncts to the cats themselves? We can't be sure, of course, but it would seem likely that two forces were at work.

Some lore traveled with the cats, for certainly when these

silken creatures of wondrous beauty were first seen by a people, many questions would be asked, and the bringer of the
cat would not in those circumstances be given to mundane
answers. When everyone around him was oohing and aah-
ing, he was likely to be spurred on to do his best; and in the
case of his owning the first cat in town, he would probably
dredge up the juiciest stuff he could remember: "In Egypt
they say . . ."; "In Greece they are said to . . ."; "Just outside
of Rome there is a temple . . ." That would be one of the
forces.

The other is far more subtle, a matter of simultaneous,
or at least parallel, invention. Some wondrous piece of lore
could originate with the sender underscoring the cat as a
treasured gift, a bearer of good fortune, a guarantor of many
healthy, noble children; and of course the promises had to be
accompanied by exotic and, yes, erotic beliefs. Nor would the
cat's reputation necessarily be wondrous. Cats do have some
qualities that are not endearing to many people. They hunt
songbirds, and a lot of people for a very long time have cared
about birds. A cat taking a prince's favorite mockingbird in
the prince's own garden would not have endeared himself to
the principality. Even killing rats and mice, although certainly the one great economic service cats can perform, has
not always been viewed as a blessing. The priests of the Greek
sun-god Apollo kept white mice as sacred animals, so one can
assume that cats would not have been their favorite animal.
The only animal not invited to the Buddha's funeral was the
cat, because when the Buddha was ill a rat (sometimes given
as a mouse) was sent to bring the medicine that would heal
the master, and a cat killed the rodent before it could accom-
plish its mission. It is a bad rap, but the cat has had to take it
in Buddhist lore for a long time. It is said that only two animals did not weep on receiving the news of Buddha's death—
the cat and the viper. Since both are mouse and rat eaters, it

remains a puzzle why people whose staple food is rice should have come down on the side of the rodent. In parts of the Roman Empire, a cat killing a bird was seen as the female element of life assaulting the male element of spirituality. But then cats have often figured in the battle of the sexes, being so fecund and so willing.

Throughout all of cat-and-mouse mythology, whenever the cat has been black it has been evil, and the mouse has almost inevitably been portrayed as white. On the other hand, and more rarely, when the cat has been white, the mouse has been black as a demonic symbol of the world.

Cats move silently, and that has variously been viewed as good and bad. Stealth is the consummate skill displayed by the hunter, and until rather recently (as time and the history of man go), 99 percent of the world's people survived only if some member of the family hunted. Hunters, unless competing with the cat for rodents or the smaller birds, have admired the cat's stealth. On the other hand, those people not having to hunt for their survival have viewed the silent approach as threatening. This may be why the cat and the terrible serpent have so often been linked in one body of lore or another, for serpents are silent too. Cats turn into snakes and back with remarkable ease throughout the world's folklore.

The cat is a collage of madness and myth, of awe and aesthetic ecstasy. From the beginning in Egypt this picture has never been simple or clearcut. It is love and hate, fear and trust, darkness and light—all the facets of the human imagination.

Study by Kuniyoshi

The cat family at home, by Kuniyoshi

8

The Cat Interpreted

IT HAS NOT been enough for us to know and love cats. Mankind has apparently always felt compelled to describe animals in terms of the emotions they engender, and the cat's silent gaze, generally signifying power and mystery, is a leitmotif in most every manifestation of human intellectual endeavor. We look back, but the cat doesn't blink, nor does it look away.

A law that originated in southern Wales in the tenth century states the value of a cat in pragmatic terms: "The worth of a cat that is killed or stolen: its head to be put downwards upon an even floor with its tail lifted upwards, and thus suspended wheat is poured about it, until the tip of its tail is covered; and that is its worth; if the corn cannot be had a milch sheep, with her lamb and her wool, is its value; if it be a cat which guards the King's barn. The worth of a common cat is four legal pence." *

In 1857 the Comtesse d'Aulnoy wrote of a white cat and gave her and her fellow felines the power of human speech, the ability to play musical instruments, and an admirable sense of decorum. The only thing that was accurate was the decorum part. Cats are not only voluptuous, they do seem to have a style that can be likened to good manners and a mysterious sense of propriety. Witness Comtesse d'Aulnoy in her "The White Cat":

> When his dress was complete, they conducted him to an apartment he had not yet seen, and which also was magnificently furnished. There was in it a table spread for a repast, and every thing upon it was of the purest gold, adorned with jewels. The Prince observed there were two covers set; and was wondering who was to be his companion, when a great number of cats marched by two and two into the room and placed themselves in an orchestra at one end of it; some had books, which contained the strangest-looking notes he had ever seen; others guitars; and one of them held a roll of paper with which he began to beat the time, while the rest played a concert of music.
>
> As he was reflecting on the wonderful things he had seen in this palace, his attention was suddenly caught by a small figure, which just then entered the room, and advanced toward him. It wore a long black veil, and was supported by two cats in mourning, and with swords by their sides; they were followed by a numerous retinue of cats, some carrying cages full of rats, and others mouse-traps full of mice.
>
> The Prince was at a loss what to think. The little figure now approached, and throwing aside her veil he beheld a most beautiful white cat: she seemed young and melancholy, and addressing herself to the Prince, she

* From *The Cat and Man*, by Gillette Grilhe, Putnam, New York, 1974.

said, "Young Prince, you are welcome; your presence
affords me the greatest pleasure."

This fairy-tale quality, this far stretch of the imagination
is evident no matter where we dip into history, where or when
we sample the human mind on the subject of cats. Is the
meeting of the white cat and the prince any more a flight of
fancy than a statue of Bastet wearing a gold earring that signifies the sun created in pre-Ptolemaic Egypt? Is either more
romantic than a hauntingly mysterious etching of a cat by
Picasso? In North Africa the cat is the incarnation of the Corn
Spirit. A piece of corn is hung behind the door to bring good
luck, and that luck is doubled if a cat nibbles the offering. Are
such beliefs—and there are scores of them—any less fanciful
than the veiled white cat and her bodyguard? Not really. For
the cat has always been a link between the possible and the
impossible. Perhaps that helps explain what has so often been
our overreaction to cats. They dare us to go beyond what we
know, to accept not only our own dreams but also those of
strangers too.

In an Egyptian papyrus a cat, symbol in this instance of
the sun, is pictured holding a knife and cutting off the head
of the evil serpent Apophis. A cat with an opposable thumb?
Why not? No more of a fiction than a cat speaking to a prince
in flawless and ever so polite French.

A story perhaps just as fanciful as that of the white cat
has traditionally been accepted as true by historians. The
Egyptians, at war with the Romans, sacrificed a major strong-
hold of a city rather than risk injuring the cats the Romans
carried onto the battlefield with them. The Romans, those
arch-cynics of history, seem to have understood their Egyptians well. Yet, for contrast, in Ypres, France, the town fool
would be sent up into a high tower to throw a cat to its death
at the start of the harvest, a barbaric custom that lasted until
about the time of World War I. Refusing to accept any single

interpretation by man, the cat defies logic and takes us on imaginary trips to and beyond the far edge of our own manageable reality. The cat is its own reality, one we have admired and feared and adored, but one we have not yet come to terms with.

Among the fables created or at least recorded by the Bewick brothers, John and Thomas, is one involving the cat as a devious conniver:

> An eagle had built her nest upon the top branches of an old oak; a cat inhabited a hole in the middle, and in the hollow part at the bottom was a sow with a whole litter of pigs. A happy neighborhood; and might have long continued so, had it not been for the wicked insinuations of the designing cat.

As the story unfolds the cat visits the eagle and tells her the sow is digging out the roots of the tree, and when the tree falls the pig will eat the eagle's young since they cannot yet fly. She then visits the sow and tells her that if she goes out, the eagle will steal her piglets to feed her young. While the cat goes out at night and finds prey, both the eagle and the pig are too terrified to leave their young alone, and soon the eagle family and the pig family die of starvation. The cat, without risk, feeds them all to her young.

It is said that in Turkey just over a century ago the typical punishment for an adultress was to be sewn into a sack with a live cat and then thrown into the sea. The barbaric beliefs represented in that bizarre custom fit well with the malignant gossip and troublemaker in the Bewick fable.

In 1870 James Anthony wrote about a generous cat that lets a rabbit go because it pleads the fate of its seven young. The cat says, "Go, and keep out of my way; for if I doesn't find something to eat, you may not get off another time. Get along, Rabbit!" Quite the opposite of the Bewick fable in its assumption, and just as fanciful in its way as the French proverb which states that if a man loves cats he is destined to marry an immoral woman. Human and inhuman, natural and unnatural, supernatural and even superhuman—the cat has suited every storyteller's needs. It has helped us realize that as long as we are not burdened with reality, we can be as unreal as we want. Fiction, sensical or nonsensical, does not come in degrees. Once we have left reality behind we might just as well keep right on going. The cat has served us well in this regard.

Have any of us grown up without hearing of "The Owl and the Pussycat," one of the most fanciful tales of a cat, and one of the most charming?

> The Owl and the Pussy-cat went to sea
>   In a beautiful pea-green boat:
> They took some honey, and plenty of money
> Wrapped up in a five pound note.
> The Owl looked up to the stars above,
>   And sang to a small guitar,
> "O lovely Pussy! O Pussy, my love,
>   What a beautiful Pussy you are,
>   You are,
>   You are!
> What a beautiful Pussy you are!"

Eventually, of course, they buy a ring from a pig and are married by the turkey who lives on the hill. We leave them dancing on the beach by the light of the moon after having dined on mince and quince using a runcible spoon. (Millions of youngsters have enjoyed this poetic fable without ever knowing or perhaps caring what a runcible spoon is. For those who do care, it is a three-pronged fork with curved tines one of which is knife-edged.)

Puss-in-Boots, of course, lures young rabbits into a carefully baited trap. Kipling wrote about "The Cat that Walked by Himself," and T. S. Eliot about a cat-about-town known as Bustopher Jones and other delightful characters that ended

up on Broadway in a musical called *Cats*. Lewis Carroll has a
cat telling a little girl named Alice who happens into Wonder-
land that "I'm mad. You're mad. We're all mad here."

These fables and many more all come back to one

The sculptor Apuy and his wife, with a cat under her chair and a kitten under his arm, Egyptian, c. 1275 B.C.

strange, contradictory set of statements: The cat is good, the cat is bad; the cat is a good omen and it is a bad omen; it is good luck and it is bad luck. Select from those associations as you will, one fact remains undeniable. The cat has an incredibly high recognition factor. That is so not just because we have, many of us, had cats around at one time or another; it is because a cat is always *more* than just around. The cat is the great insinuator. It becomes part of what we think, what we trust, what we fear, what we believe and, not just incidentally, what we are.

So firmly is the cat implanted in our consciousness, it was inevitable that man would exploit the animal for his commercial advantage. In the 1890s Hoyt's Cologne featured a cat and kittens on advertising cards that found their way into many Victorian scrapbooks. Black Cat was a stove polish, the Clark thread company used a collection of cats called "The Cat Congress" on very colorful signs in the last quarter of the last century. Dr. Thomas's Electric Oil Liniment, advertised as "Worth Its Weight in Gold," used a cat as a symbol in its advertising. Early in this century, the cat was a symbol or device for shoes (Kitty Kat shoes made by the James Clark Leather Company of St. Louis), talcum powder, patent medicines, seeds (the Salzer seed company of La Crosse, Wisconsin), Persian apples (from Washington State, not Iran; the Persian part was the cat), beauty salons (for people, not cats), and a good many brands of cigars including Two Toms, Our Kitties, Cats, Pussy, Mr. Thomas, Old Tom, Tabby, Me-Ow and White Cat. Cosmolac was a varnish produced in Brooklyn that for some reason, in its ads, featured a cat pursuing goldfish in a bowl. Collectors of Coca-Cola memorabilia cherish a 1924 ad for the soft drink featuring a stylish lady drinking Coke while watching her white cat drink milk from a pretty blue bowl.

Up until about 1930, Household Tacks from the Diamond Tack and Nail Works in Raynham, Massachusetts, featured cats on its boxes. There was a Black Cat hosiery line with the appropriate image, and a White Cat line of underwear from Wisconsin. A life-sized cat named "Tom Hidden" advertised floor coverings, cabinet hardware and house furnishings manufactured by the Otis Hidden Company. Hood's, a packager of sarsaparilla and various pills, featured "A Wedding in Catland" on a series of advertising cards, and generations of Americans have walked around on Cat's Paw heels and Cat-Tex soles.

Back in 1914 Kellogg advertised its Toasted Corn Flakes with a picture of a child holding a gray cat alongside the legend "For Kiddies Not Kitties." By the 1930s Kellogg was featuring a box-back offering of a colorful cloth doll of "Crinkle the Cat."

Chewing tobacco, soap powder, Fisk tires, gasoline, household cleaners of all sorts, the Chesapeake & Ohio Railroad, infant formulas, ink, rubbers, silverplate tableware, candy, gin, sewing-machine ribbons, roofing material, wheat flakes, lead paint, Beecham's Pills, oranges, flashlights, batteries and a great many other products all have availed themselves of our inability to ignore cats, however we may feel about them. In fact, collecting cat-packaging and advertising material is a popular hobby. The list above is from an illustrated compilation by Alice Muncaster and Ellen Yanow called *The Cat Made Me Buy It!* (Crown Publishers, 1984). Antique dealers automatically set anything aside that has a cat on it—they know that a collector will be by before long to ask for things feline, almost anything at all. And why shouldn't a cat attract the potential buyer's eye, hold his attention and perhaps lure him away from the competition? It wasn't all that long ago that people worshiped the cat symbol and even died for it.

The cat's value to the creative spirit has been more marked than perhaps that of any other animal. Aldous Huxley relates in an essay how he advised an eager young would-be writer to buy a lot of paper, pen and ink, and a pair of cats. That, according to Huxley, was the only formula he could compound for becoming a successful writer. And there have been so many situations into which our creative imaginations have plunged cats (perhaps to see how they make out) as to defy cataloguing. There is a French fable about a cat that changed into a woman. Also from France comes the fable of a cat and two sparrows, and another about a cat and a fox. Ambrose Bierce wrote about a cat and a king, and Ernest Thompson Seton (whose real name was Ernest Seton Thompson, but he didn't like his father) wrote about a cat and a monkey. Seton also paired a fox and a cat for another of his stories.

The Irish say, "Beware of people who dislike cats," a proverb echoed round the world. The Albanians seek perspective in their proverb "The cat is a lion to the mouse." The Portuguese err, if at all, on the side of the animal with "A house without either a cat or a dog is the house of a scoundrel."

Other proverbs, collected in a book called *Centuries of Cats* (Claudia de Lys and Frances Rhudy; Silvermine Publishers, 1971), include the French "For a good rat, a good cat," the Hindu "If you want to know what a tiger is like, look at a cat," the Japanese "The cat's a saint when there are no mice about," and the Russian "The day is young, said the cat, remembering that he could wait."

Pithy comments on the cat come from a variety of elegant sources. Abraham Lincoln is credited with "No matter how much the cats fight, there always seem to be plenty of kittens." Like much of Lincoln's homespun humor—and he was apparently a very funny man when he wanted to be—the remark may have stemmed from traditional frontier wisdom. Mark Twain, too, had something important to say about cats:

"If a man could be crossed with the cat, it would improve man, but it would deteriorate the cat." H. L. Mencken made the obvious observation, "Cats do not like prudent rats." George Eliot wrote, "I'm not one of those as can see the cat in the dairy, and wonder what's she's come after."

Sri Lanka, once known as Ceylon, and before that as Serendip, is not particularly nice to its feral cat population. In fact it is one of the last countries in the world where I would want to be a feral anything. Still, Sri Lanka is a Buddhist country with an amazingly rich and ancient lore. Its fairy tales are treated as wisdom and guide more than children into the world of dreams at dusk, for such lore was the written and spoken truth of people who were building magnificent cities and temples while Europeans were living in caves. In one of these stories a young monk asks permission from the Buddha to leave his side, to return to the world of his father and marry a woman with whom he had fallen in love. Buddha, who was then in one of his earlier incarnations, though well on his way to enlightenment, told the young monk of a female cat that tried to lure a cock out of a tree with the promise of marrying him. The cock resisted the temptation of the female cat and lived another day. Likening the female cat to a designing woman who would call a monk away from his vows and duties, the Buddha left the monk to make up his own mind. The young man stayed with Buddha and avoided the sirenlike call of the cat/woman.

The cat as a temptress is repeated endlessly in human lore. The cat, again, is voluptuous, and our present sexual freedom in much of the West may be directly linked to our expanding love affair with the cat. Is it coincidence that the cat population is growing at an astounding rate at the same time that we are becoming less and less self-conscious and anxious about our sexuality? I suspect not. By the same token, a fear or dislike of cats may be a projection of our fear of our natural selves. In almost every painting I have ever seen of prostitutes in a house designed for their trade (and referred to in slang as a "cathouse") there has been at least one cat. For, after all, should a prostitute fear a voluptuary?

When Paderewski made his concert debut at St. James's Theatre in London, he was terrified as he approached the piano, observing the audience staring fixedly at him. As he settled in to play his first number, a cat that lived in the theater jumped into his lap. This so delighted the audience and so charmed and calmed the brilliant young composer and pianist that he allowed the cat to remain there purring throughout the opening etude. Until his dying day Paderewski swore that the cat got him over that first hurdle.

In Japan an elderly woman approaches a temple and kneels before the wishing stone. Gently she reaches out and rubs the stone and thereby assures herself that her recently deceased cat has been admitted to heaven. A temple cat looks on and moves away to join a priest who is arranging strings of paper birds, each one of which has been contributed by a cat lover in honor of a now dead companion.

Karel Capek wrote of his cat from the cat's point of view: "Then my Man lifts me up and buries his warm face in my fur. Just then, for a second a flash of higher existence awakens in him, and he sighs with bliss and purrs something which is almost understandable. . . . But you musn't believe that I care about you. You have warmed me, and now again I shall go and listen to the dark voices."

Deus ex machina, wishing stones, higher existence, all cut from the same cloth: the magical potency of the cat. And more. For while fundamentally cats are linked to us by their needs, their affection and our love, they are also linked to "dark voices" and magic talismans (often they are talismans themselves), as are we through them—linked that is, to we know not what and perhaps dare not guess. William Butler Yeats wrote:

> Minnaloushe creeps through the grass
> Alone, important and wise,
> And lifts to the changing moon
> His changing eyes.

and therein implied that higher wisdom of the voluptuous hedonistic materialist which even the most ardent cat lover cannot deny is the essence of being a cat.

It is entirely possible to go skipping and jumping from age to age, from culture to culture, almost four thousand years' worth, and find the cat itself skipping and jumping from guise to guise, role to role. The wisest of writers, artists and thinkers have had their views of the cat, ranging from the amusing to the intensely introspective to the wildly fanciful. Ordinarily people have accepted as truth if not actual gospel the ways cats not only fit into our lives but guide us, protect us, threaten us, or at least symbolize any of these powers. Cats are imagined, on the one hand, to suck the breath from our children, and on the other to bring harvests that keep our children and us alive.

We can, in fact, have it any way we want, inasmuch as cats are so confounding they may be not only given every virtue but also accused of every sin. As for the cat and how it views all of this—the cat, remember, stares back and doesn't blink. That has to mean something. Besides, Ernest Hemingway, the apostle of masculinity in twentieth-century literature, owned forty cats. That is eighty unblinking eyes. Since Hemingway interacted with the giants of art and literature of his time so intimately, how many secrets were locked away behind those eyes?

The tomb of Madame Lesdiguieres's cat

9
Of People and Cats

CAT LOVERS like all domestic-animal enthusiasts, tend to communicate with each other about their pets. Perhaps "commune" would more accurately describe what goes on. It is perfectly clear to those of us who have taken the vows that if someone we know is not keen on cats there is no point in chatting on about how wonderful our pets are because such discourses draw a blank look at best and an open declaration of boredom at worst. But let just one cat lover find out that the enthusiasm is shared, and look out! The stories roll forth like an unraveling ball of twine. There are times, of course, when our knowledge of other people's lives with cats does not come from tales related but rather from observations made. Watching people with their cats can be revealing.

I have a friend we will call Bill. He is a successful business executive in a field that demands one-on-one contact with virtually scores of different people every week. It involves two-hour lunches and three-hour dinners and endless cocktail receptions and a great deal of domestic and international travel. Bill may have business appointments in three different cities in one day. Not all that surprisingly, Bill worries about his heart, although there have been no real signs of trouble. Bill feels the stress he lives under every day. He needs neither more money nor proof of his own skills and energy. Heaven knows what he does need—with one exception. He needs the acceptance love implies, as do we all.

Bill did not get on well with his mother, and only in recent years, as he plunges on toward middle age, has he gotten along with his father. He is at sword's point with his only sibling, a sister, and her husband. Bill never found a lady of choice, although he is very fond of ladies. Like so many extremely dynamic people with brilliant minds, large bank accounts and investment portfolios, and a personal phone book inches thick, Bill never found the time or perhaps acknowledged the need to put his private life together. He used to be a lonely man returning, I think, rather reluctantly in the evening to his expensive apartment with its breathtaking view of the New York City skyline. Bill's life was lived in a series of towers, and his footsteps there had no echo.

As he pointed out on numerous occasions, Bill likes cats. He always admired ours and spoke fondly of those he encountered in the homes of other friends. There was always an excuse, though, always a reason why he couldn't or shouldn't have one himself. After all, until the ice is broken, cats are easier to deal with as generic abstractions. The cat in the abstract—a beautiful, graceful, athletic animal. A cat, yours, is a soiled litter box, hair on the chrome coffee table, and something you have to feed and take into account if you travel. A cat, like any animal, is a commitment.

One day Bill went shopping and came upon two little kids sitting on the sidewalk in front of a market with a cardboard box between them. Kittens were spilling out of all four sides, and the youngsters scurried around on their hands and knees retrieving them. They had to find homes for them that very day. Their parents would not allow the kittens back in the house (although, typically, it had been those same parents who had failed to spay their queen and thus added to the endless flood of surplus kittens).

Although he claims not to know how or why it happened, Bill left that frantic scene with a small orange-and-white kitten who became known as Christopher. Bill has not been the same since. Christopher sleeps on Bill's bed, unless Bill has a guest for the evening, and the number of words Bill claims Christopher understands has long since passed not only the possible but the imaginable. In short, Bill has a family, including the child he always really wanted, and although there are spots in Bill's life that Christopher just can't fill, anyone who does fill those spots temporarily is regaled with the wonder of that marmalade-and-white cat. If Bill weren't such a good friend we would be tempted to threaten to leave if he told one more Christopher story, but that would be unkind. We have, however, limited him to four an evening and also put a restriction on the number of (almost always superlative) adjectives permitted.

The interesting and telling thing about this simple tale of Bill and Christopher is not how much love Bill discovered in a cat but how much love he discovered in himself. It is not just what people bring out in cats, it is, perhaps more importantly, what cats bring out in us. So very often it is the cat's role as a mirror that is so therapeutic or, just as pleasant, so recreational. It is not possible to envision Bill without a cat now, although for well over forty years he denied himself what has turned out to be very important to him. Somewhere in Bill's future back then, Christopher was always waiting. Destiny was well seen to.

Rob was raised in the heart of New York City by one parent; his father died before Rob ever really got to know him. His mother worked for the city and somehow managed to put Rob through college with shoes on his feet and books under his arm. It wasn't an easy life for either of them. Without a father, and without a brother or sister, you would think Rob would have benefited from a pet. But he never had one. Either he never asked for one or his mother wouldn't let him have one. As a young adult fresh out of a city college, Rob followed his mother's lead and got a civil service job. It wasn't enough for Rob. He was a young man with places to go and things to do. Somehow he drifted into the motion picture industry. He rose steadily, married a successful book editor, and they produced a son. Then, quite suddenly a question arose that Rob had never anticipated. His son wanted a pet. For some reason it took Rob by surprise. I remember discussing it with him. He was literally bewildered. Nothing in his own background had conditioned him to think "pet." To un-animal people like Rob a pet is like the other guy's religion. You never think about the thing in terms of your own life.

Rob was not given to denying his son anything, and quite quickly their first cat came on board. What astounded Rob above all else was that he fell madly in love with the creature —one he would never have dreamed of getting for himself. His wife claimed that Rob rushed home from work not to see her or even their son, but to see the cat. The cat became as fixed on Rob as Rob was on it. Rob had fallen into a trap. He began to need what he hadn't even known he could want.

It wasn't long before the studio head at whose home office Rob had been working in New York recognized that they had a gentleman of quality in their employ and the offer came to go West. As sometimes happens in the motion picture industry, the offer was a very substantial one, the address west of Hollywood was really good, and the size of both the pool and the car were awesome to a modestly raised New York City boy. All the flash and flourishings of his moving up rapidly through the studio ranks did nothing to lessen Rob's love for his cat. (It was his now—it had never really become his son's pet despite the original intent.)

Wherever Rob wandered—in the elaborate game room, on the patio, near the pool—the cat was always there. And therein lay the beginning of a tragedy. The routine was for Rob and his son to leave together in the morning. Rob dropped his son off at school and then went on to the studio. Very often the cat followed them out of the house and tried to get into the car. Rob's son was sent scurrying back with the cat to pop him back through the front door two mornings out of five, at least. One morning the cat did his at-your-heels routine, but wasn't noticed. While Rob's son was busy strapping himself into the right front seat, Rob slipped into the left side and slammed the door. But the door wouldn't close. Rob looked down and nearly passed out. Their cat was lying beside the car with his back broken.

A mad dash to the veterinary hospital followed by consultation with a board-certified veterinary neurologist did no good. Rob's cat was put to sleep. Rob stayed home from the studio for three days, quite literally in mourning. It was a terrible double-edged tragedy. A cat he had never dreamed he could even care about, much less love, had not only died —he himself had killed it, albeit inadvertently.

Rob's son is in school in the East, now, and Rob has had another cat or two, and once again a human being has discovered dimensions within himself, through cats, that he never knew were there. But unfortunately, trauma was involved, as it so often is when love is discovered. Unlike Bill, Rob never talks about his first cat. He can't. You can only know about his tragedy if you knew him at the time. Right after it happened he called me from California and we talked about it for a long, long-distance time. He had to then. He no longer will. I don't know how well his subsequent cats have fitted in. I suspect there never has been one like the first.

Cat lovers can be paradoxical, like all lovers. Barry and Jane are what can only be described as super-accomplishers. He is a successful surgeon, she is a world-class artist. They have four children, three of whom are already happily married. Although neither Jane nor Barry has reached sixty, they have five grandchildren. Barry has one idiosyncrasy. He likes not only saving human lives but also destroying animals. He is a big-game trophy hunter, and his office, his beach house, and his New York apartment are crammed with mounted heads interspersed with reflections of his gentler side, art. He is a gracious host, a good conversationalist and a generous friend. He is also a finely honed killer, a deadly shot with any category of firearm, who owns a collection of the best guns made anywhere in the world.

Jane goes along with this paradoxical side of Barry because there is nothing else she can do. When they are on safari he hunts and she sketches. Her sketches later become handsome art, and his skillfully placed bullets result in glass-eyed mockeries of former life.

To complete the paradox, both Barry and Jane are cat lovers. Barry would no more allow a cat of his a moment of pain than he would his own children, yet he will and has shot lion and leopard and heaven alone knows what else. As he sits by the fire in the evening swapping stories with friends, a cat is on his lap. When he walks across the floor a cat does figure eights around his ankles. No one, not even Barry, remembers how many waterfowl he has gunned from the skies or how many huge trophy animals he has brought back from Alaska, Africa and Asia. Nor, in all likelihood, could he readily recall how many cats he has loved.

I have never understood how a person can love a Siamese cat and spend days trying to kill a lion or a leopard, or any other wild animal for that matter. The obvious contradictions defy analysis. I once asked Barry, and he just shrugged. Perhaps, one day, their cats will complete the job they have started—the domestication of Barry. In the meantime they live very pampered lives and travel between two luxurious residences in a fine European motor car. They probably don't recognize their distant cousins on the wall. I wonder if Barry does.

One of the most extraordinary cat lovers I have known was also one of the first I came to know. I met him through a nurse-housekeeper my parents hired named Mabel Sarah Helena Moore. A doting spinster who quickly became my second mother, Mabel Moore had me to herself on some weekends and made off with me by bus and train to Newburyport, Massachusetts. There, in an old settlement, lived Mr. Robert E. Lull and his housekeeper, Mabel's mother. Mrs. Moore baked the most incredible pies in anticipation of our visits, and Mr. Lull, unquestionably one of the most fascinating men who ever lived, had the history of the world ready to share with me. I would rather have spent ten minutes with Mr. Lull than have been in the world's largest candy store during a power failure.

Robert E. Lull was a renowned book and autograph dealer, a historian and a cat lover. He was an ancient man when I was a small boy, and in 1938 he still dressed the way he had in 1894. He wore a detachable celluloid collar with a black string tie. His shirt cuffs, too, were detachable celluloid,

るつ名仕立あけらる
　　　　ろくりらあと
ひとくの布を
　　　よらせてぬりさん

挑花園・義人

朩のそれの
　ころを仕らる
　　　　ろくりらまた
朩下の
　　やみの
　　　星ねりまして

村農屋　鈴成

A woman sewing, and her cat, by Kuniyoshi

十三

花咲庵
采守

and were protected by green cotton slip-ons that went from his wrists to his elbows and kept his shirt-sleeves clean. He wore a green visor to protect his eyes from overhead glare as they peered out from behind gold-rimmed glasses that gave him a distinctly owl-like look, a nice owl-like look.

After checking to be certain my hands were clean, he would sit me down on a large black leather couch with a tufted back that soared over my head, then would place a folder on my lap. On one occasion it would be a folder with a letter written by every president who had served up to that time—up to Herbert Hoover, I would guess. Another time it would be the prime ministers of England, the kings of France or the signers of the Declaration of Independence. The fact that I collect books and autographs to this day undoubtedly began back then.

There were fixtures there in Mr. Lull's incredible inner sanctum. Cats, always cats. One curled up in the big leather chair beside me and seemingly listened as Mr. Lull regaled me with the wonders of history. Another cat slept on a pile of correspondence on his desk, and others took their leisure on piles of books or boxes of books and manuscripts recently retrieved from some cellar or attic and not yet examined. It was a magical place. Gentle Mr. Lull seemed to know all about everything that had ever happened, and he spoke of long-dead artists, scientists, and world leaders as if they were old friends. In a way, I guess they were. The sun came through the old handmade windowpanes with their bubbles in that crooked old New England house so bursting with wonder, and motes of dust moved gently through the slanting rays that illuminated patches of wide-plank flooring. Cats— as pleasant and appropriate to the setting as Mr. Lull himself —shared it all. I will always insist that they looked wiser than most cats I have known, even wiser than my own beloved

Michael. Cats seem to belong where scholars sit and ponder greatness. Occasionally they wash their faces, they stretch from time to time, but mostly they doze and listen. I listened and have been a history buff to this day. History and cats meld in my mind; they belong together.

Mr. Lull is surely long gone now. I saw him last about a half a century ago. His cats, of course, are gone too. But when I see a painting of a pope or a saint or a scholar with a cat at his feet, I think of Mr. Lull. If they could have talked together, those great people and Mr. Lull, one of the things they would have talked about would have been their cats. In their gentleness and their greatness, they would have known about cats just as the Egyptians did. Great people know all about wisdom, and for four thousand years wisdom has included communion with the cat.

Many of the most successful and powerful men in history, along with a good many businessmen today, have been or are notoriously inaccessible—to all but their cats. Men and women who can barely fit into their schedules their most important peers and colleagues always are available to their cats. Their cats understand the problems they have, they don't criticize, and they have an uncanny instinct for finding the niche of the moment and filling it with quiet grace, appropriate playfulness and calm. I suspect cats have heard more great secrets than have any other animals in history. A cat's discretion is never in doubt. A cat's approval is never to be questioned. And cats sit as tall as a king, like those who shared Mr. Lull's desk. Cats demand that time spent with them be quiet and reflective time. They are the ultimate placebo. Someday I shall name a cat "Valium."

One of the most poignant stories of a cat and its role relationship to a human that I ever heard came about as the result of a near-tragic mystery. Friends of ours in a suburb of

Boston have only one child who survived infancy. Never was
a child more wanted, more adored than Bobby. He was handsome and bright and cheerful and had just about everything
a boy could want as he entered his teen-age years. Then,
slowly at first but at an ever increasing rate, Bobby entered a
world of dark shadows and overwhelming melancholy. His
work went from worse to terrible at school, and his friends
fell away one at a time. The boy was lonely, apparently
frightened, and a pall of gloom seemed to have settled over
him. He was being drawn down by an inexorable and as yet
unidentified force.

Bobby's parents realized that help was needed, and the
boy was placed under the care of a psychiatrist. School and
interaction with his peers were now out of the question. But
even with constant care and drug therapy the boy unaccount-
ably continued to regress. He was approaching a catatonic
state with the likelihood that his still unexplained downhill
slide might never be reversed.

At fourteen Bobby could not feed himself nor see to his
own toilet. In another two months he stopped talking and
entered a six-month-long tunnel of darkness and silence.
Halfway through that darkest period the therapists ceased getting eye movement from him. He was frozen inside his own
mind, and the specialists who came through had no explanation and held little hope.

The only glimmer was that Bobby would respond slightly
in special circumstances. He would move his eyes when
shown a picture of a cat. He would not talk, not even in a
grunt, there was no facial expression, but he would move his
eyes when pictures of cats were passed before his face.

At one point in his childhood he had had a pet cat, and
it was decided that bringing in a live cat might make a difference now.

On a day well planned in advance, with his doctors and parents watching from behind a one-way window, a technician brought Bobby into a small examining room, seated him like the automaton he was in a straight wooden chair, then put a kitten in his lap. After a few moments Bobby tipped his head forward and looked down at the cat. Several minutes later he raised his hand in a voluntary action that had had no parallel for months, hesitated, and then petted the cat. Some time later he tipped his head to the side, and this time there was a flicker of expression—not quite a smile, but something of recognition and reaction. His parents, standing behind the trick glass with Bobby's doctor, hugged each other and wept. After more than an hour alone with cat, Bobby talked to it. His voice was flat, his speech monosyllabic—but this was an amazing giant step forward.

For nearly two and a half months Bobby's therapy consisted of daily sessions with the kitten. Then he was able to talk to his doctor.

Today, Bobby is in prep school. No one knows anything more about the dreadful thing that caused his severe regression and his near-fatal plunge into a well of lonely despair. He took, I am sure, ten years off his parents' lives, and he is in the medical literature. The last I heard of Bobby was that the school waived one of its most rigid rules. Bobby was allowed to bring a pet to live in his dormitory room with him. It was, I believe, a cat he had met as a kitten.

There is a claim, usually put forward by people not enthusiastic about animals, that cat lovers sometimes go too far in their infatuation. This is in part true.

There is a woman I have never met who has, despite my discouraging her, written to me often. There comes a point in one's life when one really can't accommodate too many pen pals.

This woman has a cat. So much for that, except that her cat is, it seems, a reliable judge of human beings, particularly those of the male persuasion. This woman must be fairly attractive, for if one is to believe her letters she often meets men who are fairly wild to know her better. She invites them home to meet her mother and her cat. The cat tells her whether to cut it off there or to move forward into a deeper relationship. One has to ask, Does her cat tell her whether she has hit gold or dust? Whatever the answer, if there is one, it must be a terrible blow for an ardent young man to be sent packing because Poopsy turned her paw down. I should think by the time matters got to that point a young man would be about ready to start packing on his own initiative.

It certainly is true that cats have a remarkable ability to judge the people they meet, but I have always believed such judgments to be feline-centric. The people judged might not be ideal friends for cats, but that hardly means they would be poor friends for people as well.

The claim of these less-than-enthusiastic people does raise an interesting point, though. Do some of us get too "silly" about our pets?

Study by Kuniyoshi

Thanatology, a relatively new branch of the science of human behavior, deals with death and how we handle it. Very often we don't handle it well, ill-equipped as we often are—especially when it is our animals we grieve for.

My mother-in-law was raised in Edwardian England. She went to a fine school "For the Daughters of Gentlemen." Her grandfather was a headmaster of a famous boys' school, and Phyllis Langdon Barclay grew up among good books, intelligent conversation and incredible British emotional stamina. She also grew up an animal lover. As a matter of fact, my wife and I gave her an African safari (non-hunting, of course) for her eightieth birthday. She went again, at her own expense, at the age of eighty-two.

Not very long ago a marmalade-colored Persian cat that was Phyllis's favorite had to be put to sleep. There was no other way. The cat had been sick for months and no hope was given for his future.

On the day Fidel died, Phyllis was found sobbing in the sunroom looking out over the water and some swans that were raising their young there. "How silly I am," said Phyllis. "How very silly. He was only a cat, after all, but I did love him so."

And that really says it all about the absurd dilemma our way of life has given us. Why should it be silly to grieve? Thanatology addresses itself to that point. It is impossible to say how much damage we have done to ourselves by being unwilling to let go, to expess our grief. Whatever possesses us to teach our children that it is "silly" or even bad to acknowledge emotions? Too many cat lovers have dreaded criticism by their peers for spending too much money to save a cat, or for openly expressing grief when their cat dies.

What about the accusation that people replace other people with cats? If they cannot relate in a wholesome, fulfill-

ing way to others of their own species, so the accusation goes,
they pick on cats to fill the void. I suppose that is true in some
cases, but I have yet to find anything wrong with it. If cats
help some people to stay on course, keep them from the dread
feeling of loneliness or of not being needed or wanted, whatever else do we have the right to expect of them?

People who do not need pets, or who cannot admit that
they need cats, find some kind of strange relief in being anti-
pet or, specifically, anti-cat. I have known people who never
had children who claim that they do not like kids, just as I
have known childless people, some married, some single, who
love kids. Why should their attitudes be different with animals? Still, cats seem to dredge up strange combinations of
emotions—the fear of cats, the dread of cats, the hatred of
cats, the adoration of cats—and a little good old-fashioned
indifference would be refreshing. It certainly would be easier
on cats than the other more high-strung emotional packages.

But there is another side of the coin when discussing the
relationship of people and cats. This is the darker side, one of
madness and cruelty, without the safeguards of law, and
where the "rights" of cats don't exist.

Not very long ago I was invited to visit a shelter in New
Jersey where animals that have been abused are kept, repaired as well as possible, and, when the opportunity arises,
placed in good new homes. It is a labor born of true devotion,
for many of the cases are dreadful. One cat, I recall, had
been owned by a woman who kept one cat at a time, presumably as a pet, and used it for a target as she practiced with her
BB gun. When the cat finally died she replaced it with another—pet. She was found out, and her last cat, still alive,
was confiscated. It had had both eyes shot out. The woman
was obviously insane, but that didn't stop her from owning
a cat.

Another cat had been used for archery practice but had lived. She had had two arrows sticking through her when rescued. The punishment available for such human monsters is less than for shoplifting a bagel. All kinds of laws protect these maniacs, but virtually no meaningful ones protect the cat. The situation is so lopsided that future civilized people may wonder how we ourselves survived or, perhaps, how we survive each other.

The big problem is that anyone, no matter how weird they are, how savage, can get an animal, and very often he selects a cat. Dr. Mengele at Auschwitz could always get subjects for his insane practices. Maniacs in our society can, too.

Animals in America have virtually no rights at all. They are recognized as property and can be killed at the owner's will. If it were otherwise, farmers could not send their cattle, sheep and hogs to market, and pet owners could not ask a veterinarian to put their ailing pet to sleep. One suspects that animals will always be property, but perhaps we can find a way of giving them rights. A lot of people are working on that right now, although they have not made any major progress that I know of. There are difficult legal, philosophical and ethical questions involved. How do you give real rights and protection to an animal while maintaining it as property? Cruelty-to-animals laws seldom affect the people who are really cruel because the savagery they indulge in occurs behind closed doors. We can only guess at how many cats are locked into a scene like the one with the madwoman and her pellet gun. No one hears their cries. It is silent anguish in a nightmare world. Few search warrants are issued to seek that world out.

In an earlier chapter we spoke of the cruelty that is part of cat lore throughout history and most of the world. The problem is, you don't have to dwell only in the past, or go much farther than, say, the house down the block. On Long

Island, New York, I live near a dear old man whose name doesn't really matter. He is close to ninety now and still operates a farm with all kinds of livestock. He keeps the farm going because he loves children, and his institution, for such it has become, gives kids an opportunity to work on a farm and learn farm chores. It is a lovely thing for this very old man to do, and his stock is extremely well cared for. My own son was one of his laborers learning the work ethic there when he was twelve or thirteen.

But this nice old man whom everyone hereabouts calls "Uncle" has a thing about cats. He will not have them spayed, and he lets them have kittens in the barn, under the porch, anywhere they want to. He flatly refuses to interfere or let anyone else do so. When the cat population gets too big he collects a bunch of the younger ones, puts them in a burlap sack along with some heavy rocks, and drops the lot in the pond. I have talked to him, his other neighbors have talked to him. What is to be done? That is the way farmers have traditionally disposed of surplus cats—they drown them. Which is not to suggest that all farmers do that, of course, but too many have, and too many still do, for the cats' peace of mind or mine.

Not terribly long ago a local humane society asked me to go with one of their workers and try to reason with a very unreasonable woman. It was an errand for fools. She has that strange syndrome some lonely people get whereby they come to believe that only they know how to be kind to cats and dogs. They become insanely possessive of them, steal them, and although the animals soon outnumber the coins in their purse they still insist that unless the animals are in *their care* they will be in danger. It reaches bizarre proportions, with sometimes hundreds of animals forced to live in horrible conditions.

One such lady was reported in the next town, and a

couple of us went there to bargain with her to release the animals, or at least most of them, to a humane organization where veterinary care could be obtained and proper diet managed. Every other stair in the old building's creaking staircase was broken through. Pressing against the wall, we finally made our way up to where the stench was coming from. Inside the apartment was one three-legged wooden chair and a stove that did not work. There was no electricity and no running water. There was a pile of rags the cats used for a toilet, as they had every inch of floor in that hellhole, including where the woman slept. She was in rags herself and began taking them off in some kind of weird striptease as soon as we entered. Hollow-eyed, dying cats, many of them almost totally furless from mange, peered out at us from every corner, from under all kinds of rubbish piled around the room. The smell was unbelievable. Soon the woman was naked, and it was quite evident as she cavorted around in her mad ballet that she had not bathed in months. She was terribly malnourished. There was no reasoning with her. She believed she took beautiful care of her cats. She flitted around the room scooping up a cat whenever she could catch one, telling us its name. It might be bald and its eyes might be sealed shut with exudate, but the woman asked us to inspect it at close hand and see how well she cared for her pets. How could she possibly be expected to trust anyone else to do as well if she gave them up? Reason was a senseless pursuit under the circumstances.

We left. The authorities took her into their care finally and had her hospitalized. A veterinarian was paid to go up and euthanize all of the cats. He found many dead ones under the newspapers in one of the rooms. Disease and starvation had gotten to the cats before he could help them. Not one could be saved.

And even had the woman lived on there for another

decade with dead cats piling up around her, she would still not have known what cruelty she wrought. The hitch is that the woman loved cats, and probably had all her life. In her earlier years she probably took good care of a few cats, but as she became progressively more disturbed, more and more cats were sucked into her whirlpool of madness with her. How many hundreds of cats she killed with her insane love cannot be estimated. There must have been close to fifty cats still alive there that day.

It could be argued that the woman, should a choice be necessary, deserved at least as much sympathy as her cats. She was hopelessly sick by any standards. But thousands of people like her cause suffering in tens of thousands of animal victims and frequently go unreached for years. Society fails them no less than their victims.

Too often in dealing with cases like this, volunteers and authorities are faced with shattered human minds that cannot be reached. We have two others like that woman near our town right now. Collectively they have killed hundreds and perhaps thousands of cats and dogs between them.

Ask any health department, any department of social services, any humane organization, or any police department how many times they have had to close in on people like the lady I visited. Some are not quite as bad and some are far worse. Some have BB guns and other devices of their own design.

Cats have always been especially vulnerable because they are small and essentially trusting animals. They also can't make enough noise to alert neighbors who just might care. It is not hard to lure a cat into such a terrible trap, for the cat can't always tell in time what it is getting into. Someone says, "Nice kitty," offers a food treat or water on a hot day, scratches the cat under the chin and picks it up, and from that point the cat is entirely at the person's mercy. If cats were only as independent and aloof as so many unknowing people have said they are, they might be able to stay clear of such deadfalls and dungeons. They aren't and they can't. They are forever easy marks.

We have spoken throughout this book of the worst cruelty visited on cats by man: our toleration of feline reproductive physiology. Why should it be necessary to spay and neuter cats in civilization, so to speak, but not in the wild? No one spays and neuters *Felis libyca* in the wilds of North America and the Middle East, so why their descendents? The answer seems simple enough until you give it even a cursory examination. It all hinges on how and where cats fit in.

Wild species of cats are born into environments that have natural hazards and a fixed food supply. The cats fit in exactly where they belong, as is true of all other wild animals. Where this is not true, where the cat does not fill an exact niche in the ongoing system, the cat disappears as a bad design. It has either become extinct as a species or been extirpated in that part of its range where it is out of step. This is natural selection in the sense that the animal either fits in and functions as it was meant to do or it vanishes. It is what is meant by the generally misunderstood term "survival of the fittest."

In wild populations of truly wild animals there is some exchange with neighboring areas, and if all the wildcats of a single species do die off in an area there will be a vacuum for a time—and nature will always try to fill a vacuum. But if cats of the vanished species drift into that vacuum again, they will bring the same skills that were there before and meet the same challenges. It will still be a bad fit for all the same reasons. The species in that place under those conditions will fail again. But like a pond that has become choked with exotic weeds, that vacuum, too, fills up in time with other animal life and the cats of that maladapted species stop trying to fit back in. There can be no overpopulation because the system is self-limiting, self-managing.

Only when man sticks his toe into the pool do the ripples start and we hear of animals starving to death at such a rate that they have to be hunted. What man has done, of course, is remove the natural enemies of the animals he wants to hunt—his beloved target species. He becomes the only real hazard allowed in the system. Without natural enemies, animals do overpopulate, do starve, and do die in unnatural numbers, all because they have been allowed or forced to live in unnatural numbers. No system is in charge because man has destroyed the system. (Man is never a system; he is a user or, most often, a misuser.)

Now, compare that situation with the case of the domestic cat, the god-animal we have been celebrating. The cat is transported to a place—a city, suburb or rural area where its only natural enemies are diseases (for most of which we give it shots), a few exceptionally hostile dogs, and moving vehicles—along with the odd maniac that occurs in our midst from time to time. We feed our cats, we house them, we try to keep them from harm, and almost all the kittens in a litter grow up to be cats. In the wild the lioness, as an example, almost never manages to raise more than half her cubs. But it is unusual for a normal domestic cat with a normal litter and typical home care to lose anywhere near half her kittens. They all grow up where there are no predators to speak of. They mature at about ten months, and then they can all breed new litters. It is automatic. Try projecting that. Take six kittens as the average surviving litter.

Two kittens breed at ten months and have a litter of six kittens. In ten months all of those six kittens find mates and breed. We now have thirty-six kittens that soon become cats.

And so it goes. At thirty months two hundred and sixteen, at forty months one thousand two hundred and ninety-six new cats. In five years it is forty-six thousand six hundred and fifty-six new cats. And this is figuring only on each cat's breeding once during the five years—which is nonsense with unaltered animals. Two will, in fact, become hundreds of thousands in less than a decade, even with natural attrition.

What happens to this surplus? We kill them. Some are killed by cars because they have become street cats. Some are tortured because the ideal environment for feral dogs and cats is low-density, badly decayed urban housing—the deadliest slums where derelicts and unconfined mental cases live in vacant buildings considered unfit for human habitation. That is where most of the cats and dogs go; that is where they are least likely to be picked up by authorities; and that is where they die by the countless thousands. All of this because cat lovers will not spay and neuter their hopelessly promiscuous pets.

The old bromide that ". . . we found a good home for every kitten" is pure nonsense. No cat *finds* a home—it uses up a home. In shelters all across America literally millions of cats and kittens sit in cages waiting either for an eager new family and a home or, more likely, a needle full of a barbital formula. Or worse. If you allow your cat to have kittens and place those kittens in six new homes, six other cats are not going to make it out of that shelter. Simple math. They are going to be destroyed to make room for tomorrow's influx.

The flood never stops. I visited the pound in Gary, Indiana, and the cats there never even made it inside the door. They are assembled in bags and cartons outside and killed without ever being examined or evaluated. The situation may be better now since we did a television show about the horror there, but that is not so unusual a situation. In one town in

Wisconsin the police took the surplus dogs and cats to the town dump, turned them loose and used them for target practice. It was not at all unusual for a dog or cat to show up back in town with a leg or its lower jaw shot away. Back to the dump the troublemaker went.

If we ever do have that surplus under control, what can we possibly do about the mad people in our own society who torture and maim or simply neglect the cats they so easily come by? The ideal will come, of course, only when it is difficult to get cats and dogs, only when they are recognized as the special creatures they are and saved for the people who pass muster, people who can demonstrate that they deserve not only to purchase a license for their pet but also one for themselves. Someday, when Utopia is here, license for pet owners will be required, and pets will go only to responsible people who can get such a license.

Veterinary medicine and the pet-food manufacturers have been very good to our cats. Feline panleukopenia, leukemia and many of the other diseases that used to kill so many cats are now held at bay by simple inoculations. Rabies need no longer threaten our companion animals, and even as I write, people are lining up at veterinary clinics across America to get that long-dreamed-of feline leukemia shot. Urinary tract problems, often acute and deadly, are being closed in on. Veterinary dermatologists are solving many old problems that used to be considered without solution. Dr. Mark Allan, former dean of School of Veterinary Medicine of the University of Pennsylvania, proposed two such changes during his years in that position of leadership. He suggested that aseptic surgical techniques be used on animals as well as people, and thereby he saved millions of animals from ghastly postoperative infection and death; he also proposed board certification for veterinary specialists, and now we have urologists, cardiologists, nutritionists, dermatologists, orthopedic surgeons, neurologists and many more. Things are looking up for our feline companions. The diseases have been whittled down one by one, and soon there will be relatively few left, and perhaps someday, none.

Good health is no longer a vague wish we have for our pets—we can deliver it now. Many cat foods are balanced diets, and the cans and boxes they come in carry more valuable nutritional information than do most labels we find attached to our own foods. The pet-food industry has come a long way, and our pets can now live longer, healthier lives.

Few things about today's companion cats cause even the most intense cat lovers as much distress as the fact that our cats still hunt. We all know they don't have to, but all the same we must recognize that they are killers, and that we have never been able, or perhaps have never wanted, to breed it out of them. It comes with the original package. (I am not sure we could breed it out of them even if we tried.)

Any writer or commentator on animals is bound to be asked scores of times what can be done to keep the family cat from stalking the family canary, or to keep it away from the neighbor's bird feeder. The latter problem is easy to solve: Keep the cat at home. The canary is a tougher issue because most of us don't want to turn our homes into a complex of cells with submarinelike battle-station doors all dogged down and catproofed. Your cat likes to have the run of the house just as you do, and if there are hamsters or canaries or parakeets about, then the law of the jungle takes over, usually. In effect, you have set the cat up, not to mention the animals it wants to prey upon.

We have all seen photos in our local newspapers showing

a cat nursing baby rabbits or lovingly protecting baby chicks, but those cats are exceptional, and you can't ever depend on having or training one. When your kitten stalks and pounces on a piece of string or ribbon you drag across the floor, it is preparing for bigger and better prey. It honestly doesn't know how not to. Moving objects of pounceable size turn a cat into a whole new demonic mode. (You notice, dogs chase cars while cats do not; cats are smart enough to know what is prey

Cat with a bird, Japanese

size and what is not.) They are literally possessed when offered bait. Their eyes go hard, their muscles tighten, their
nerves become like banjo strings. It is a physical reaction, so
don't think evil of the cat. If it had a choice it would still kill.
Unable to feel sympathy, it does feel a tingling sensation and
responds to it. When certain visual and audio signals are present, the cat does an almost instant transformation, abandons
the cushion and the fire, and becomes primed for the kill. All

of its hormones, all of its mind and fiber are taken over. The cat is literally overwhelmed.

In the Caras household we have birds as pets. Their cages are flight-size and catproof. Our bird feeders are out of a cat's reach, and nothing entertains our cats more than watching a busy day at the seed trays and tubes . . . from behind the glass. We call it cat television. They gather and watch and, I am sure, think rotten thoughts.

I hate it when a cat shows up on our doorstep with a chipmunk or a garter snake, but I don't hate the cat. I don't like to find the corpse of a mole on my pillow, and I am saddened when I step out the front door and find the four little white feet of a former field mouse and nothing more, or the head of a black-capped chickadee. Our cats aren't hungry, ever, but they are cats, and that means they simply have to kill. Obviously, the reason so many feral cats make it on their own is that they are such effective hunters. I just wish they didn't enjoy it. No ducking the issue, cats are recreational killers. But so are twenty-five million hunters in this country, and a lot of trappers besides. We forgive them, at least some of us do, so why should we not forgive our cats?

I dwell on this issue because so many people do have problems with it. It takes determination and resolve, a very large heart, and a tolerant twist of mind to love a cat despite the fact that it does something most of us dislike, this slaughter of the innocent.

It will be a very long time before it changes, after a great deal of genetic engineering. Then, in all likelihood, our cats will have ceased to be cats. I can't imagine what they will be like, or what we will call them. In the meantime, if you do have a cat who is not interested in chipmunks, moles and canaries, it isn't because your cat is nicer than other cats—it is just lazier. Enjoy his (or her) benign manner while you can.

Sure as shooting, your next cat will make Attila the Hun seem like Florence Nightingale.

Our almost four-thousand-year-long love affair with cats has been a kind of standoff. They have loved us, we have loved them, each of us in our own way, and we both have gained immeasurably thereby. Not many of us have eaten cat meat, almost no one has worn a cat coat (it is, fortunately, not a warm or a long-wearing fur), and cats have not provided power on the farm. Cats don't guard our homes or work well as cattle drovers—though they do kill the odd mouse or rat, and we like that, unless they deposit their triumphs on our pillows. But cats have helped us keep our blood pressure down—they are less expensive than drugs and work as well. Cats are decorative, amusing, pleasing in every way. Their popularity has never been greater than it is at this moment, and the supplies and materials to keep them well and happy are big business. There are some rough spots that need ironing out, but the problems have been identified and we are tackling them.

I have no doubt that we will have another four thousand great years with cats on our cushions, and then another and then another. As for the things cats know that we wish we knew, someday they may share that wonderful, arcane knowledge with us. I only hope, when revelation comes, that we will be worthy. The things on a cat's mind must be wonderful beyond imagining. If that were not so, would we have given them positions from gods to devils, trying to coerce them into revealing what is there? So perhaps one day it will indeed prove to have been worth it all, even for those holdouts who have not yet found it so. As an optimist, I place the emphasis on *yet*.

Cat washing itself, by Gottfried Mind, 18th century

10
Cats in My Life

ANYONE WHO has owned many cats in long succession can define his or her life as a series of furry episodes, even eras. There are many other factors in our lives, of course, but somehow cats manage to imprint our times with their personalities. Obviously, wives and husbands, children and dentists do no less, nor, for that matter, do dogs. Still, if we cat lovers are so inclined, we can look back and remember life as one big hairball, or a succession of them, if you will, one rolling on inexorably toward the next. It is restful to do so. It makes one smile even when the smile is bittersweet, as it so often is. Cats with their short lives are the very stuff of bittersweet affairs.

Cat number one in my life takes me back to Methuen, Massachusetts, about thirty-two miles northwest of Boston on the New Hampshire state line. I can even remember his name and approximate breed. We called him Michael, and he was approximately a Maine Coon cat. That would have been 1931 or 1932, about as far back as I can remember anything, when I was between three and four.

We also had a Boston terrier then, but everyone had a Boston terrier then, particularly if they lived near Boston. The dog's name was Bozo. Michael and Bozo were a pair, a piece of work in the vernacular. Michael appeared to be very nearly as big as his canine companion. They ate out of the same dish, used the same water bowl and slept together all snuggled up in a ball. That is a lot more than I can say for my seven-year-old brother and myself. We competed for center stage. Michael and Bozo were far more secure with each other. Together they explored and possessed the world.

Michael had an incredible capacity for getting into scrapes and somehow, against all odds, surviving them. If ever a cat had nine lives it was that hard-luck tabby brown-and-white, fluffy country cat. He got into some kind of grease, I remember, and had to be shaved. I can only imagine how much his ego suffered, for he was very vain. By then I would have been six or seven. Every part of him was shaved except his head and ears, and Michael went into hiding. On those few occasions during his hairless period when he was in the house, an encounter with him was always startling. There would be his great big wonderfully fully-furred head peering around the corner, and then the rest of him would enter, a very little body and neck. It was really obscene. He looked as if he were waiting to be stuffed and roasted. We shouldn't have laughed at him, but we did.

Michael went down to the river behind our house and somehow managed to get a fishhook through his cheek. It wasn't really all that big a surgical problem, and my mother managed it at home. She just cut off the shank and pushed the rest of the hook on through. Never, I learned, try to pull a fishhook out. Always continue it on its way. Michael sulked but Michael survived—as he was to do more than once.

Michael nearly got himself done in by a car. Then he had a run-in with a brutish German shepherd who was not at all keen on cats. Next he tangled with an itinerant tom who was passing through our neighborhood and who outweighed Michael by an unhealthy margin. That meant stitches. He lost one eye in that scrape but managed very well without it for the rest of his life. Somehow, month in and month out, year in and year out, Michael was always getting repaired. He was a scarred old curmudgeon by the time the veterinarian said it was time. As I recall, it was a urinary-tract problem that did him in. Michael must have been about ten years old, because we moved to Boston not long after his death, just before World War II.

Michael was a cat with infinite tolerance. He never scratched any one of us three boys, as I recall. When Bozo went on to greener pastures a collie came on board. He didn't last very long sadly, because our neighbor decided, without warning anyone, to put out poison bait for the rats that sometimes worked their way up through the fields from the river to our street. A wirehaired fox terrier was next, and Michael took him in stride; he also put him in his place—that is, he taught him the finer points a dog has to know if he is to share his turf with a cat. A cat stands for very little nonsense. At this time I thought of myself as more of a dog person than a cat person, but Michael was special.

It is easy to see why kids are very often dog people at first. A dog's life is built around what the kids are doing—baseball, walks in the woods, stick-throwing—while most cats consider their own appointed rounds of paramount concern: a mouse run here, a mole run there, a good shrewing area or a bird's nest or a place where garter snakes go to sun themselves. These all have to be seen to every day, and the kids won't accommodate their own schedule to the cat's concerns. So the kids and dogs go one way and the cats another. That is the way it is in the country. Still, a great cat like Michael will be sitting on the doorstep waiting for you to come home when the walk or game or fishing expedition is over—though only if he has taken care of his own thing. It has nothing to do with independence. It is a matter of priorities.

One thing that makes me remember Michael so clearly is something that happened after we moved from Hampshire Circle to Pleasant Circle; both are rather nice residential areas about three quarters of a mile apart in the town of Methuen. This was still before we made the big jump to Boston.

Michael had gone his way by then, and I missed him a lot after the move. Pleasant Circle was a little eerie; in fact, it was magical. Directly across the street from us was a huge castle. There were several in town. People of obviously phenomenal wealth had had the great mansions dismantled in England or Scotland and had them moved, numbered brick by numbered brick, to Methuen. At some places the walls surrounding them were eighteen feet high, and at places ten to twelve feet thick. In our new house, the room I shared with my younger brother looked out barely over the wall of "our" castle, with a glimpse of the woods and the manicured walks that led up the hill to the brooding mansion. On many evenings I scrunched down in front of the window and looked out when the moon was bright and wondered what went on up there in the castle, who had lived in it before it came to Methuen, and why, in Methuen, its American owners had felt the need for such vast walls. It was a place where a young imagination could go fairly wild.

In our yard was a rather splendid doghouse that was an exact replica of our own house. It really was a work of considerable skill. One evening as I was looking out across the wall toward the castle, imagining heaven alone knows what wondrous scene, something caught my attention near the doghouse, something in its shadow cast by the almost full moon. The thing moved, and then it stepped out into the moonlit area on the grass. It was Michael! I whispered his name. I was certainly old enough to know what "dead" meant, and I knew that Michael had been in that category for months. Yet—it *was* Michael. Now what you have to know is that Michael had a very distinct star-shaped white splotch on his chest. There was really no mistaking it, and it lay against a field of very deep chocolatey-brown tabby-brindle. I had never seen another cat with just that color fur or just that size and shape white mark. So it had to have been Michael. Yet it couldn't have been Michael. I never saw him or "it" again, but that late-night, moonlit encounter has colored my view of cats ever since. No wonder they were worshiped, no wonder people who needed to conquer a world dreaded them, no wonder kings and queens allowed them to be tortured and burned!

We did not stay long at Pleasant Circle before the move to the big city. There, in an apartment, our livestock was cut back drastically—no snakes, no turtles or birds. There was Peter, an English cocker spaniel and one of the dearest dogs I have ever known, and Sally.

Sally was a relatively nondescript cat, a marmalade-and-white job that was found during a torrential spring downpour by Mabel Sarah Helena Moore, our sainted housekeeper and nursemaid who had moved with us from Methuen. Whither we went, Mabel went. She had a terrific soft spot for animals, and poor, sopping Sally obviously with nowhere to go came on board. She and Peter sniffed each other curiously, then settled in together and were soon doing what Michael and Bozo had done—one water dish, one food dish, and a couple of good places to snuggle. Since Englewood Avenue, where we lived, tended to have its share of Boston-bound traffic in the morning and suburb bound in the evening, and since we lived on a curve, Sally was confined. She still went out to make her toilet, but "out" for her was a balcony three levels above the street.

Sally did one thing that bothered me no end. I had a brown-and-white hooded Swedish laboratory rat named Fibrinogen, Fibby for short, of whom I was extremely fond. She was an immaculate little creature who liked to curl up in a dry mop for her nap. Peter accepted Fibrinogen without any reservations. She was a Caras critter and as such had her rights, one of which was not to be eaten. But Sally was another story, or so it seemed. Never did she lay so much as a paw on Fibby, but she wanted to, oh, did she want to! So Sally stalked Fibby. Whenever Fibby was abroad, even when she was riding on Peter's back, as she often was (she bathed twice as long after touching poor Peter, for clearly he did not meet her standards for hygiene), Sally was on patrol. No matter where Fibby went, Sally was not far behind, cross-eyed as a bat and making oddly humming, twittering sounds in her excitement. Good Lord, Sally could look evil. There is no doubt she wanted to pounce and have a bit of filet of rat, but something in her understood the terms of living in our house: Leave everybody else alone. Still, Sally made us nervous, to the point where Fibby was never out unless well guarded. There would be Sally, cross-eyed and scrunched down looking like death itself, ready to strike down the innocent. In a way, I suppose we were tormenting her, though all we saw it as at the time was Fibrinogen's right to a constitutional—a right that was apparently driving Sally mad.

Studies for the fifty-three stages of the Tokaido,
by Kuniyoshi

Well, Sally outlived Fibrinogen without having done our littlest beast any harm. And then began my time in the wilderness, my time without pets.

First there was Army hitch number one. I did manage to catch and keep for a while a pet snake at Camp Polk (now Fort Polk), Louisiana, at least until the other guys in the barracks found out about it and threatened to get me the next time we went to the rifle range. And I did find some homeless cats in an unused section of the base that I could feed and visit. But not touch; these were dragons, living on their own as long as they apparently had. I once saw one dragging off a large copperhead, holding the struggling snake by the head. They were tough cats, all right, and I never so much as touched one of them, although in some strange way I considered them mine. Years later I would work with tigers and lions, bobcats and cougars, and even, on one occasion, a leopard, but none of them came close to those cats at Camp Polk for sheer orneriness.

After the Army there was an intense duel with zoology at Northeastern, then Western Reserve University in Cleveland (not yet Case-Western Reserve), then Tufts College back in Massachusetts, then back into the Army for another hitch, then the University of Southern California. It was of necessity a petless time for a wandering soul. It felt strange being without animals, but I got used to it. Not having a cat or dog is an impoverished way to live. No one should have to do it.

After USC it was back to New York City, where I had to share an apartment with a fellow allergic to nearly everything but corned beef, tuna and me. No pets again. But then there was Jill. She had been percolating through my psyche ever since I had met her when she was sixteen. Jill was even a less-controlled animal lover than I was, so I guess it was inevitable. When Josef Erich von Stroheim, son of the great film director, had introduced us he had predicted marriage. Three

years later he was proved right, and we two animal nuts
hitched up the wagon and headed for our own apartment.
We had no pets. Her Boston terrier, Pixie, was at home with
her parents in Boston, and her last cat had just died.

One evening Jill and I were walking to a theater along
West Fifty-sixth Street in Manhattan. As we passed a
darkened entryway a very plump alley cat appeared and began
doing figure eights around our ankles, purring impressively.
Clearly this was an act of communication. The cat was trying
desperately to tell us something. We had no choice but to
listen. The cat simply would not let us pass. It would do a
figure eight, run into the entryway, then come back out to do
another turn with our ankles. "She wants you to let her in,"
postulated Jill. "Hmmmm," I answered sagely as I followed
the animal into the small dark area separated from the lighted
stairs beyond by a glass door. The door was locked, and as I
was about to pick a bell, any bell, and get the door clicked
open, I noticed that the cat's problem was not ingress but
nourishment. Someone had put out an expensive can of
white chicken meat (in natural broth) but had not run the
can opener completely around the track. The top had been
left hinged on and somehow had gotten pushed back down.
A little of the broth had seeped around the edges, but the
Fifty-sixth Street cat couldn't get at the meat that so tempted
and taunted her—at least not without help. I drew the trusty
blade of my penknife that had seen me through so many
hangnails and otherwise unopenable cartons and pried the lid
back out of the cat's way. She launched herself at that
chicken as if that far too expensive treat were her inalienable
right. Judging from her condition, something of equal value,
if not chicken, was hers on a regular basis. Chicken isn't all
that nourishing for a cat, so I suspect that this was in fact
treat day.

And people say cats aren't intelligent! Here was a cat with

a problem, and she (the gender is a guess) figured out that she could not solve it alone. But she knew there were two-legged creatures on her planet who could solve it, who could be enlisted in her service. So she headed out and picked her marks—Jill and me—and managed to convey to us that she needed our help. The cat solved her problem by creating another problem she felt she could handle—to find someone to attend to the first problem. She did and we did and Jill and I walked on toward the theater convinced it was time to end our suffering—we had to get a cat.

Caras family cat number one was Thai Lin, a most excellent Siamese with one of the most finely honed senses of decorum I have ever encountered, in man *or* beast. A wild thing as a kitten, Thai Lin matured into a gorgeous seal point with a rank libido. She howled and yowled, and it began to dawn on us that we couldn't live with her unless she was spayed.

So, Thai Lin was spayed, and became ever so much more pleasant to live with after surgery. She seemed to be totally unaware of the missing parts, and I like to think she welcomed her time of peace as much as we did.

From the beginning Thai Lin homed in on Jill. She was nice enough to me, in fact, she was dearly affectionate, an ever-present lap-sitter, but she was Jill's cat and was not embarrassed in the slightest that I know it. She fussed when Jill was out and was even worse when Jill came home, scolding her as she moved at her heels from room to room. "How dare you stay away so long," was clearly what she was saying. Thai Lin's voice stopped barely short of breaking wineglasses.

Not very long after Thai Lin took possession of Jill, we were walking down a drive near a stone wall one evening when we heard the most pitiful wailing from the woods beyond. I climbed over the wall (elected for the task because I was so agile then) and found what was left of a litter of kittens that had been tossed there in a burlap sack to die. Three of the kittens in the sack were dead and a fourth was near death. The survivor was jet black and about as big as a minute. She bit me and then, obviously in heartfelt appreciation for my having saved her life, scratched me as I carried her to the wall and over it. I don't think she had been handled very much.

We got the waif home and Jill bottle-fed her and let her sleep in a cardboard box with a hot-water bottle piled with towels. She became Eartha Kat and turned out to be another retarded cat. She and Thai Lin had a brief period of hissing and spitting, but that passed and Eartha assumed her role as Caras Family Critter Number Two.

Eartha was probably our least memorable cat. She was never really affectionate, although from time to time she would try a lap for a bit. When you petted her she bumped your face with her cheek to mark you, then went her way. Being really dumb and having had a terrible start in life had marked her. Still, she was ours and we had accepted responsibility to help her lead a good life as long as that might be. It is not written, after all, that all pets must be brilliant or even charming. We often have drab brothers and sisters and, God knows, we have dull aunts and uncles. Why shouldn't an occasional pet fall short of the mark? That is no excuse to dump them. Besides, our other pets may find them enchanting.

On one occasion when we were moving into a new place, we temporarily lodged our cats at my in-laws' apartment. I stopped by for lunch one day and wandered into the bedroom. My in-laws' apartment was on the seventh floor and the bedroom had a triple window arrangement. The center window was six feet wide and did not open. There were two two-foot end windows that did crank open. There was dumb

Eartha in the middle of the six foot window, outside on a very narrow ledge, obviously trying to glue herself to the glass. She had gotten out one of the side vent windows that for some reason was without its screen. I could not reach Eartha from either end. Had I tried, she surely would have fallen. The only thing I could do was approach the situation as quietly as possible and coax her to keep coming in the direction she was already facing. After all, she had already gotten halfway across that terrible six feet. As I walked toward the window Eartha decided to turn around, and as I watched in horror, she vanished over the edge. She actually had more than seven floors to fall, since directly below was a cement ramp leading to the basement service entrance. I was sure Eartha was dead. (Cats do land on their feet, but they can tolerate a fall from only relatively small heights. Idiots who toss cats off roofs to see them land on their feet should be chucked off after them so we can see them land on their heads. One act makes as much sense as the other.)

Etching by Edouard Manet

I came out of the bedroom with a look that could not have been mistaken for anything but catastrophe. Jill and I got in the elevator and went down to collect poor Eartha's remains. But there she was down at the bottom of the ramp, eight floors below the window ledge, looking dazed and sore, but clearly alive. There was a metal canopy over a window several floors down, and she must have bounced off it and broken her fall enough to enable her to survive a plunge that would otherwise have killed her. She moaned as I carried her upstairs and got her onto a cushion. Her gums showed poor capillary return, indicating shock. We got her to a veterinarian; countless X rays revealed no parts broken or out of place. Eartha did a lot of sleeping on soft pillows, but she got better. Now we are very careful about windows in our apartment, even though all of our cats live at our house in the country and are almost all smarter than Eartha.

Eventually Eartha got out the back door of our house and vanished. We looked for her for days, but there never was a sign of her. I would rather know a pet is dead than wonder if it is trapped and suffering. We never did know about Eartha. Poor thing, she was always so vague. I am sure her end, however it came, puzzled her. Everything else in life did.

The day came when our daughter Pamela was born, and, as far as Thai Lin was concerned, that was it for Jill. I have never seen a cat drop someone faster. Or go for a new person more quickly. The moment that infant entered the house, she was all there was for that cat this side of Jupiter. Thai Lin was so insistent upon getting into Pamela's room that we finally had to put up a screen door with a hook and eye so we could hear our daughter and not worry about Thai Lin leaping on her. The nonsense about cats sucking the breath out of babies is just that—nonsense—but a cat will out of curiosity or maternal instinct jump up to where an infant is and snuggle it or wash it. The snuggling and washing are harmless enough, but landing on a sleeping child can startle it, and almost certainly isn't good for it. Still, at every opportunity, there was Thai Lin helping to change diapers, helping to bathe and feed Pamela. She could attend to nothing else. All of her other chores were neglected. In all her world, all that mattered for Thai Lin was one infant girl named Pamela.

Thai Lin's appearance had by now changed slightly. When Eartha joined us she had brought along ear mites and had passed them on to Thai Lin. Thai Lin had scratched and scratched her ears until she finally broke a blood vessel in one of them and it became as thick as a deck of playing cards. The veterinarian had to operate. The practice at the time was to sew a large button on the ear, then tape it back against the cat's head. I am not sure what the button was supposed to do, but in Thai Lin's case the cartilage was broken and the ear never moved up to its natural perky position again. She remained for the rest of her life a lop-eared cat.

No matter. It didn't bother her and it didn't bother us, and as Pamela grew into her playpen and then into a toddler, wonky-eared Thai Lin was always at hand. Pamela teethed on Thai Lin's good ear, pulled her tail and tried to see why Thai Lin's eyes wouldn't come out, but Thai Lin didn't mind. She just purred louder. She may have been a spayed cat doomed forever to maidenhood, but in Pamela she had found her outlet. She was the Earth Mother, giver of warmth, the eternal security blanket. When Pamela began talking, she told us she had two mothers, "Mummy and Thai Lin." Thai Lin concurred. Eartha, then still around, looked vague about it all.

When Pamela went to school Thai Lin sulked until her "child" got home, then scolded her for being away, just as she had Jill years before after her longer absences. Pamela dressed Thai Lin up, pushed her around in a doll carriage and slept with her cat on guard every night. No matter what time we went into her room to check on our daughter we could be sure of one thing: Thai Lin would be curled up on Pamela's bed with her front paws folded in under her creamy breast, purring with her eyes half closed. She would watch us as we adjusted the covers or pillow, watch us as we left the room and softly closed the door, and then she would have Pamela to herself for the rest of the night. It was as things were meant to be. Bastet had ordered it so. Thai Lin purred.

In time—three years after Pamela, to be exact—our son Clay came along, and although Thai Lin thought it was dandy having two kinds of kids around the house, it was still Pamela above all others. She retained a warm spot for Jill and for me, I am sure, but nothing like the one she had for the child who now shared all secrets with her. It was a grand relationship, the kind that gives our childhoods their texture and our memories their depth.

Life has its ways of taking sharp turns, and for Pamela and Thai Lin such a turn came when Pamela was nine. We decided to spend some time living in London—good friends Stanley Kubrick and Arthur C. Clarke were going to make a film called *2001: A Space Odyssey*, and I had been invited to join the production—and Thai Lin simply couldn't go. British quarantine restrictions had become impossible, prompted by their fear of getting rabies back, now that they had eliminated it from the United Kingdom. A dog or cat had to remain in quarantine for six months, and that long in a cage didn't seem to us an act of love. So Thai Lin and Eartha, it was decided, were to live with Jill's parents, who were spending more and more time in our country house anyway. Thai Lin wouldn't be uprooted so much as she would be deprived—Pamela was being taken away from her. Pamela worried about it, lost sleep over it, and shared her mounting grief with us as the time for our departure neared.

What made it especially hard was that Pamela was mourning, not just anticipating a temporary separation. She said over and over that Thai Lin would die if she went away. She just knew it, somehow, knew that her cat would not survive without her, that in fact she wouldn't want to.

In time we settled into a small house on Hollycroft Avenue in Hampstead Heath, just north of London. We were again petless, although a great yellow Labrador retriever named Joss who lived nearby took up with the kids and drank most of the milk they were given. Still, a pet of their own would have been nice. And Christmas was approaching.

We knew of a famed Siamese breeder outside of London named Mrs. Dunhill. Her cats were rumored to be the best ever, so we called her. She said she might be able to help us, making it very clear that that could only be if we passed muster. She was not promising to sell one of her kittens to any stranger on the phone, particularly one with a dreadful American accent.

We drove out on a miserably rainy Sunday. Mrs. Dunhill eyed us carefully and brought out a perfectly horrible five-month-old Siamese that hissed and spit and yowled at being held. No chance, even Mrs. Dunhill saw that, and passed the beast off to a cattery assistant. We had tea and talked for a while, and Mrs. Dunhill admitted that the cat she had shown us was not one of her own. She was helping a friend get rid of a litter (of *Tyrannosaurus rex?* I was tempted to ask). But nine-year-old Pamela and six-year-old Clay were charming, and Mrs. Dunhill softened up over tea, after which she brought out Sumfun Abigail. Now there was a true Dunhill Siamese: beautiful, calm, gentle, a near-perfect cat. Her grandmother, Ninna, we were told, was the heroine in Keith Bryant's book *A Kitten for Christmas* and a half sister to the cat in Sir John Smythe's lovely *Beloved Cat*. Evidently only the best and brightest people knew enough to have one of Mrs. Dunhill's cats.

We made our deal, although Mrs. Dunhill was not keen on one of her best creations leaving England. We described the idyllic life her kitten would lead when eventually we returned to the Colonies, and made our way back to Hampstead, Abigail along. I was shaking from a bone-breaking brand of British flu, and with the sleet and the rain, Jill was driving as well as she could, given my moaning and Abigail's meowing. We made it alive—in my case, barely—but the important thing was that by the time we got home, cold and shivering, a remarkable creature named Abigail had somehow become a part of our lives.

We anticipated terrible problems back home if this new Siamese cat were to become especially attached to Pamela. But as it turned out, while both Pamela and Clay enjoyed their Christmas present enormously, Pamela understood, and never allowed herself to become the focus of Abigail's attention. Abigail slept on our bed, not Pamela's, an arrangement we made sure of by the judicious use of open and closed doors. We were determined to head off trouble before it arose. Pamela had stopped mourning Thai Lin's anticipated death, but she was still worried about her, and the flow of letters from home failed to reassure her. It was always in the back of her mind that she had abandoned her closest friend.

The situation was probably helped by the addition to our household of an exceedingly strange trio of pets. We were making 2001 at the MGM studios in Borehamwood in Hertfordshire. One of the crew had been on location with another film in Africa earlier in the year and had come home with three bush babies, small nocturnal pre-monkey primates (pre-monkey, that is, in that they are farther down the scale than monkeys, actually among the lorises and not far from the lemurs. They are, however, clearly primates like us except they have bushy tails and weigh about as much as a postage stamp). This film person had all three bush babies in a terrible little cage, and they were not well. Their tails had gone all bare. I bought them from him out of pity, and that is how Patrick, Broderick, and Fredrick, "the Ick brothers," joined our menagerie.

Bush babies can be fiercely threatening little devils, and they bounce around like rubber balls. Abigail (we had dropped Sumfun as being a bit too cutesy) loved the bush babies. They threatened her by going up on their hind legs and spreading their arms wide while hissing like komodo lizards. Abigail thought that was just swell. She could spend hours getting the bouncing bush babies to do their threat displays. The spectacle never ceased to amaze her—or us, for that matter.

Spring came, the bush babies had furry tails again, and Abigail had grown into a great beauty. Fortunately, she was still clearly Jill's cat. The time was nearing for our return to the states, and Pamela and Clay began packing their many London-acquired possessions. The plan was for Jill, the kids and the animals to sail home on the *France*, and I would follow a month later by plane. Three days before they were to sail, the cable arrived. Thai Lin had died. It was a terrible moment for Pamela, however convinced she had been of its coming—and then the most extraordinary thing happened. That very night, instead of coming to our room as she always had, Abigail went to Pamela's room, jumped up on her bed and snuggled up. And, just as Thai Lin had done, she abandoned Jill. She became, on the day we learned of Thai Lin's death, Pamela's cat.

Anyone who has owned cats and dogs has had such things happen, or knows of them happening to other people, but who can explain them? How did that cat know? What, if any, message was sent by the tone of Pamela's voice, or Jill's, or mine? Was it body posture or was it something else?

Michael had been long dead when I saw him walking in the moonlight, with the castle in the distant background, and Thai Lin lay dead a hemisphere away when Abigail somehow knew there was no longer any problem with rivalry and gave herself for the rest of her life to lonely, needy, catless Pamela. Who can say how these things work?

Once we were settled back in the United States the influx of animals picked up. Whether we were at our New York apartment or our country house, there always seemed to be cats and dogs in trouble, animals that simply could not be left to die. Nell, a mixed-up random-bred German shepherd-type dog, came into the fold from the streets of New York. She was to last for sixteen years. She loved cats.

I was asked to do a publicity job for a shelter near our house and while we were there Jill spotted a tiny fur ball in a cage with a pile of dried cat food near it. An idiotic sign had been penciled on a card and stuck to the cage door. It read, "See if she can eat." Presumably, if she couldn't, the idea was to chuck her out with the rubbish. The kitten was far too small to handle the tough dry food; she needed baby food that was soft and nourishing.

Daisy was instantly adopted and is still with us, now the oldest animal we have of the approximately twenty in residence. She is also one of the most hopelessly spoiled animals on earth. She still looks like a kitten, although she is well up in her teens. She is also a constant liar. The moment anyone goes into the kitchen, she is at their ankles fibbing about how many days it has been since she was fed. Every night before I go to bed I say out loud, "Daisy, did they forget to feed you today?" and she appears like magic telling me that that is indeed the case. At meal times she stands on her hind legs and taps me on the thigh—literally, *tap-tap-tap* with that furry little paw—to remind me that she is near death from starvation. If we have guests, she gets up on a side table and taps them on the shoulder—*tap-tap-tap*, I am dying. Daisy is devoted to milk and beef, lamb, chicken, turkey, ham, pork, eggs, anything delicatessen—in short, to virtually all foods. She is no bigger than a minute under her glorious gray-and-white coat, but food remains Daisy's overwhelming passion. She also likes to be carried, held and petted, and is totally indifferent to the other cats and dogs that have come and gone during her lifetime here. She is a fey, quiet, gentle creature who would like to eat twenty-four hours a day. I wish I were like her. She never puts on weight.

Then Meep joined the herd. I don't remember where big old tabby Meep came from. (When you have lots of cats you tend to forget where they all came from.) His peculiarity? When he was tiny he stuck his muzzle into another cat's bowl of milk and inhaled. The milk went up his nostrils instead of into his mouth, and he never liked bowls of milk again. Yet he loved milk. Since Pamela and Clay would occasionally leave a few drops at the bottom of their glasses, Meep had a means to solve his problem. He would daintily dip his paw into the glass, then lick the milk off his foot. Even when offered a bowl of milk he used the lick-the-paw technique. Eventually the kids stopped giving him bowls of milk and set aside a small glass that became known as Meep's glass. He would get his glass of milk and dip and lick to his heart's content. Fortunately he was a right-pawed cat—and his right paw had snow-white fur for its front one-third. He was an immaculate cat.

About milk—no cat or any other mammal (including us)

really needs it once weaned. Yet most cats love milk, and as long as it doesn't upset a diet of properly balanced ingredients and doesn't give them diarrhea it is a fine way of letting your cats know you love them. It is, however, a treat, not a basic food once the kittens go onto solid fare. In nature no weaned cat would ever have a way of getting milk, and lions and tigers grow up very well, as we know.

Amanda Blake, the lovely lady who played Miss Kitty on *Gunsmoke* for just short of twenty years, is a hopeless animal person just as Jill and I are. She comes to visit often, and from the start Clay recognized her as a soft touch. If he knew of a cat that needed help, he would hold it in reserve and the moment Amanda arrived for one of her regular visits he would spring it on her. The cat got a home immediately, and Amanda had rude things to say about kids who ambushed her. She says there have been more ambushes staged in our house than there ever were in Dodge City.

On one such visit Clay popped a marmalade cat on Amanda, pleading that it was facing imminent death. Amanda headed back west a few days later with Little Clay (sic) in his pretty new cat carrier and a ribbon around his neck—blue, of course. We all knew he was going to love it in Phoenix, where Amanda was living at the time and where Little Clay promptly had several kittens. Clearly a mistake had been made, but that small orange cat, now spayed, currently lives in Los Angeles with Amanda, and is still known as Little Clay.

Things have a way of coming full circle, however. Clay eventually went to work at a veterinary hospital, and while there he witnessed a terrible confrontation. A woman brought in a tiny snow-white ball of fur and, asserting that the cat was deaf, asked the veterinarian to destroy it. It had blue eyes as well as white fur. It was obviously a purebred

Angora. The gene for blue eyes in cats does carry that recessive characteristic for deafness, and in this case, as in X number of times per thousand it had surfaced. The veterinarian refused to kill the kitten, and Clay scooped it up and brought it home, ". . . just until we can find a home for it." How many times had we heard that one? Of course the animal stayed on, and in an inspired moment of retaliation Clay named her (sic!) Amanda. And of course when it came time to have her spayed the veterinarian parted her fur and—long hair can be confusing—castrated him instead. Amanda became Mr. Amanda, which he is to this day. Now there is a cat with peculiarities!

Mr. Amanda is not only deaf, he is quite retarded. We hope and believe that he leads a rich internal life because not a heck of a lot goes on outside of him that he notices. He sits and looks at you with a blank stare and then, very often, will walk toward you. He will stop halfway, stand for a moment with his head cocked to one side, then execute a perfect somersault, then faint. He will recover, think that he has done something grand, somersault and faint again. Sometimes he just faints without first executing his gymnastics. He seems to enjoy all this.

Poor, vague Mr. Amanda isn't a terribly neat cat. No hair balls for him—he relies on others to take care of his coat. He has remained a kind of soiled yellow snow color all of his life, except every now and then when someone gives way to despair and plunks him into a tub of water. He comes out snow-white and spitting angry. The anger soon passes, as does the snowy look. Soon he is yellow-and-brown-on-white again (unless he has gotten under a car, in which case he is black-and-white-and-greasy).

One particularly steep set of stairs here at the house has a metal banister that offers little in the way of footing. Mr. Amanda regularly tries to go down it backwards, inevitably slips and falls and, of course, faints. When he comes to, he tries it again with precisely the same results. All those knocks on the head can't have helped him over the years.

We once had a glorious bulldog named Pudge who ran to the front door with enormous enthusiasm whenever a walk was in the offing. Mr. Amanda always seemed to get in the way when the sixty-pound behemoth went slamming toward the door. Time and again Mr. Amanda got run over, and naturally, he always fainted.

Still, Clay was right to save his life. Even Mr. Amanda's strange internalized existence and his frequent bouts with unconsciousness and the fact that he has never heard anyone say "Nice kitty" or ever heard a dog bark at him is better than being dead at seven weeks of age. Mr. Amanda is as safe as such a flake can be in our home, and he is welcome to stay as long as he lives. But he is getting on in years, and I wish there was some way we could convince him to forgo the banister trick. The other cats and dogs always stare at him. They must think it strange too.

Etching by Edouard Manet

Kate the Good is another cat with amazing qualities. She is what is variously known on different sides of the Atlantic as a colorpoint shorthair, a lynx-point Siamese or a tabby-point Siamese. Whatever, she is a Siamese, and she is a marvelous-looking cat. The day I took Kate the Good on television with me one morning ("Good Morning America"—ABC) with her friend the late Jeremy Boob, a golden retriever, I had thirty-five phone calls and innumerable letters later offering her the opportunity of a new home. Kate the Good was another rescue case. It is strange that so many people believe that shelters and pounds have only random-bred dogs and cats to offer. In fact, they have just about every imaginable breed of cat and dog as well. There is certainly nothing wrong with random-bred pets, but if you do have a hunger for a purebred animal of one breed or another, just visit enough shelters often enough and you will find what you want.

Kate the Good is the cleanest cat, I am sure, that ever lived. She bathes herself endlessly. Not only that, she bathes everybody else. If a strange dog comes into our house, Kate the Good performs an immediate laying on of the tongue. It would never occur to her to bite or scratch or make rude sounds. She will walk up to anything—human, cat or dog— and start licking. Our other cats think it is glorious to stretch out on a soft cushion under a warm lamp and have Kate the Good cater to them from head to foot. It gets to the point of bordering on the obscene, like a scene from *Caligula*. The dogs love it, too, but that's a problem. We have four blood-hounds, and for Kate the Good, even with her advanced level of hygienic skill, to lick a one-hundred-and-forty-pound bloodhound stem to stern—just one, let alone four—takes forever. We are sure she will injure her tongue, but she continues to insist that no one knows clean but her, and to demand that everything that lives come up to her high standards. Except for one. She has given up on Mr. Amanda. He must taste awful, what with all the things he gets into. And he isn't very grateful. So Kate passes him by and starts on a far less needy cat.

Another visit to the shelter turned up a super purebred Persian in the most incredible apricot color I have ever seen. It just didn't seem real. It turned out that this very valuable cat belonged to one of the wealthiest and best-known families in America, but the lady of the household had developed a ferocious allergy to all animals. The family presented the cat to a good shelter with a substantial donation for his care until a suitable home could be found.

Fidel moved in and lasted for years, but then he developed so many allergies of his own that it became almost impossible to feed him. The problem was compounded by the fact that our other cats are fed at least two meals a day from a large communal feeding tray, and for Fidel, who always managed to get some of it, that food was death itself. He was a perfectly loving cat and a great beauty, but he had more dermatological problems than the Elephant Man, so after a national deficit's worth of veterinary bills and allergy tests, the curse that brought Fidel to us took him away to where everything is safe to eat. It was a sad parting. He really was a terribly nice guy, but he was beyond help.

Xnard (pronounced Snard) is a happier case. He is a gray-and-white cat who is perhaps the most contented creature on earth, which is all the more amazing when you consider his origins as one of two male cats, brothers, owned by some idiot "heads" in Boston. The said idiots force-fed LSD to both Xnard and his brother, and finally Xnard's brother went out a ten-story window to his death. This all took place near the Boston University campus, where Clay spent his undergraduate as well as medical-school years, and when

Clay learned of it he made his way to the place and announced that Xnard was leaving. None of the heads saw fit to
challenge the six-foot-two student with the red beard, and
after Xnard had gone cold turkey in Clay's Boston apartment,
he came to us on Long Island. It is almost as if that little cat
(he did not grow up to be very large) thanks the sun each
morning because no one is still force-feeding him drugs. He
is as happy as a cat can be. (What happened to Xnard goes
on much more than most people realize. Drug users do force
drugs on their pets, and although that is not as bad as getting
the stuff into the hands of youngsters, I would still suggest
capital punishment for first offenders. It would cut down
markedly on second offenders.)

Eventually our cat population rose to thirteen, and that
was not only unlucky, it was unwise. Even ten cats in one
place has invited the scourge of feline leukemia, a terrible
disease, as we came to know firsthand. (Just as this is being
written, a vaccine for feline leukemia is becoming available,
and in future years no cat owners will have to worry about
this killer.)

Our thirteenth cat was a kitten brought to us, of course,
in desperate need of a home, and we took it in, as so often
before, "until we can find a good home for it."

The kitten was clearly a carrier of a very hot strain of the
leukemia virus. In short order we lost great Meep, the milk-
on-the-paw licker, and six others. The kitten died and took
seven of our cats with her. It was like London during the
reign of Charles II. The plague struck, and we had to stand
by and wait helplessly for the next cat to die. It was a sad time
for everyone, for each of us lost a favorite including Abigail,
Mrs. Dunhill's very special Siamese from England. Waiting,
just waiting to see who will be the next to sicken and die, is a
very helpless feeling. There was nothing we could do—the

harm had been done. All of our cats in residence had been exposed, and only five were able to develop immunity.

After that grim nadir, we acquired one of the most remarkable cats to have come our way. We knew there was something strange about him from the start, but since he was already full-grown and of unknown origins, we could not be sure of anything. Something about his appearance made us call him Rufus: the scientific name for the North American bobcat is *Lynx rufus*. He had a bobtail which the veterinarian examined with great care and declared was his normal tail— the terminal caudal vertebrae were present. Hmmmm, a very, very large cat with a natural bobtail. He carried this abbreviated tail straight up in the air and flicked it just like bobcats do. He also had ear tufts, although he was tabby-and-white in color. He liked to play in water. Strange for a domestic cat! He sat in front of the water dish and drew pictures on the surface with his paw. Sometimes he walked right through it. His front legs were almost twice as thick, at least the bones were, as those of even a large ordinary cat. He weighed close to thirty pounds. The mystery deepened. His

Etching by Edouard Manet

shoulders felt like a quarterback's, and he had a ruff of fur around his face. He also had a very strong odor, just like the one you might encounter in the cathouse at the zoo. I have held a few socialized bobcats in my time, and they had the same smell. Very pungent, very wild.

Finally, Amanda Blake dropped by for a few days. "That animal is a hybrid," she declared. "He is just like our bobcat." Amanda and her former husband, Frank Gilbert, were the first private citizens in America to break the cheetah-breeding code (polyandry—one female plus several males) and breed the animals in captivity. They had a large wild-feline compound in Phoenix, and bobcats were among the cats they maintained there.

Further checking revealed the fact that someone in the Middle West had been breeding domestic cat/bobcat hybrids, so there was the chance that Rufus was the product of their strange hobby. I called Allan Eckert, author of the book *Crossbreed*, a book about a cat like Rufus, and he asked a number of questions and confirmed what the veterinarian, Amanda Blake, Jill and I were sure of: Rufus was a half-'n'-half cat.

We have no idea where Rufus came from or what had happened to him in his early life, but he did spend the better part of a year in a cage in a shelter, which was where we found him. Why he wasn't adopted sooner I can't for the life of me imagine. We got at least one offer a month from people willing to "take him off your hands." No way. Rufus had found his home. When he arrived, he did not want to be touched, much less held and restrained. Then he did a complete about-face. He hopped into any handy lap and purred his strange bobcat purr. (That was another clue, that *ummm-hummm-strumm* purr that just didn't sound like a domestic cat's at all.)

Rufus got up in the morning and walked through the house. He zonked every dog and cat he met, just to remind them the king was up and around. He had been declawed, so no one got hurt, though sometimes Mr. Amanda used a swat from Rufus as a reason to faint.

On declawing . . . I have never heard a subject involving animals with more nonsense attached to it. Go to any shelter and you will find cage after cage of cats with signs on them that say, "*Claws Furniture.*" These cats have been turned in because their owners could not wean them over to scratching posts. They have little if any chance of being adopted, so eventually they are "put to sleep," the common euphemism for "killed." It happens tens of thousands of times a year. It is silly, cruel and needless. Jill and I collect antiques and art as well as animals, and understandably we have some pieces we wouldn't want to see in tatters. With all the cats we've owned, we have had to monitor that situation rather carefully. Some of our cats would not use a rug-covered log or post, no matter how much catnip we put on and around it. Rather than cage the animal—terrible for a cat—or get rid of it, we have had to have a few of our cats declawed.

A good many self-styled "humane" people have made an anti-declawing campaign their life's work, and they are quite foolish, frankly. The vision of some sadistic veterinarian tearing the cat's claws out with pliers as the animal screams in agony is just not true. The animal is fully anesthetized (the procedure is often combined with spaying or neutering to spare the animal an extra anesthesia experience) and only the first bones bearing the attachments to the claws on the front feet are removed. Stitches are generally used, one or perhaps two for each toe, and the animal goes home that night. Why people think it is right to remove a male cat's testicles and wipe out his sex life (it is not only right but essential in virtually all cases) and wrong to remove its front claws rather than kill the animal, I cannot imagine. Spaying, again a social responsibility, is actually a far more serious procedure than declawing.

For the record, cats do not claw drapes and furniture to "sharpen" their claws, as is usually stated. They are peeling away the old outer sheath of their claws to make room for the new claws growing underneath. Can declawed cats still defend themselves? Yes, indeed they can. When a cat is in trouble it doesn't use its front claws as much as its hind claws: a cat rolls onto its back and rakes its adversary with its hind feet. And a declawed cat still has its hind claws intact. Can a cat without front claws still climb trees if it has to? Yes, almost always. I have seen those of our cats that have had to be declawed run up trees many times and lodge well out of harm's way. They go up and down trees the way we do stairs.

We do not suggest that declawing be a regular procedure like spaying and neutering (which certainly should be)—but when you have just had a Victorian couch recovered in an authentic fabric for fifteen hundred dollars and you would like it to stay intact at least until the dinner party on Saturday, declawing is an option that is both humane and rational.

Anyway, Rufus had been declawed, and he still ruled over a houseful of cats and dogs.

He had one very peculiar habit that I have never seen in another cat, and I can find no explanation for it. If you scratched Rufus on the back, just forward of the base of his tail, he made a strange licking movement and craved metal. He was in heaven if you let him stand on your lap while you scratched him in the prescribed area and simultaneously gave him a ring or watch to lick and nibble at. In the absence of those items he would chew on a shirt button or a brooch if you happened to be wearing one. But his favorites seemed to be wedding rings and gold watches. He never scratched them with his teeth; he just liked to lick them and hook his teeth under them. I can't imagine what licking gold is a symptom of, but my wife has something close to it. You don't have to scratch her back to turn her onto gold, however.

Down in our laundry much of the time is Harriet Winston, a Siamese. At the time she came on board as a sad derelict we had a beagle puppy someone had abandoned in a local Caldor parking lot. We had named the pup Tiffany, and it seemed nice to have a Harry Winston to go with a Tiffany. But everything went wrong. A friend came to dinner and refused to leave without Tiffany. Love had struck like a tsunami and that was that. Then we found we had done the Mr. Amanda/Little Clay thing again, and Harry Winston became, quickly and quietly, Harriet Winston, now without a Tiffany to play bookends with. The tale of Harriet's background is rather sad. For fifteen years she had belonged to an elderly couple. One of the couple passed away and the other member had to be hospitalized, which proved to be a permanent arrangement. Everyone forgot about poor Harriet (or whatever she was called then). She had been locked up in a shuttered house for over a week without food and water when some distant family member remembered her and took her to a shelter. We took her in, but at fifteen she really didn't want to mingle with other cats and dogs. So she has her own cat box, her own water dish, and is fed alone. She has a basket she loves to curl up in, and the other animals of the household have by now all satisfied their curiosity about her and leave her in peace. At her age she really should not have had to adjust to yet another family, but she knows she can stay with us as long as she lives. She isn't anyone's special pet, which is sad, but she is safe and warm and blissfully antisocial.

Clothild is just a plain opportunist. There is no other word for her. She is shameless. A weird-looking tricolored female somewhat large for a lady cat appeared on our doorstep one day, and when she was still there the next morning we fed her—a fatal mistake with strange cats and dogs. She stayed, of course, eventually moved in, and at first appeared happy. Then she disappeared just as suddenly as she had first appeared. She was gone for months, then there she was again in perfect coat. Obviously she has at least one other home.

This has gone on for years. Clothild the User comes and goes at intervals of several months. We have never had a clue as to where her other home or homes might be, but she never looks run-down, and she certainly isn't surviving out in the woods on her own. Clothild the User lives by her wits, and we have no choice—when she shows up we feed her. She does enjoy being warm and dry, and she is pleasant with people and reasonably tolerant of other animals. Kate the Good bathes her.

There are other cats like Clothild. They live in the country and have several homes staked out. They know just how to work their deals, which has to suggest a high level of intelligence in cats (or a low level in humans). The Clothilds of the world always get by. Ours doesn't offer an awful lot in return except the opportunity for the people she uses to feel good about how humane they are. It is a neat gambit, and a lot of people try to adopt it. They are never as good at it as cats.

Tom was a big black cat with lots of scars on his pudgy face, suggesting that he had had more than one disagreement in his life with others of his species. He was a big, tough hombre. One day my wife opened the front door to let our resident cats know that dinner was served. In they all trooped, and shortly Jill did a double take as there, by golly, was an

Study by Kuniyoshi

extra cat snuggled down next to the food tray with our gang. They didn't seem to mind, and as far as we were concerned, one more mouth didn't matter that much. But our other cats' acceptance was odd, since cats are generally not all that keen to find strangers on their turf. We had to assume they all knew the big, powerful handsome stranger rather well. He got called Tom and attached himself like a limpet to Pamela, who was home from college. He hung around, dogging (catting?) Pamela's footsteps, and then, when she went off to college again, Tom vanished as suddenly as he had appeared. Nothing more was thought of it.

Two weeks later Pamela was scheduled to come home for a weekend. As she drove up to our house, Tom was sitting in the driveway waiting for her. We had not seen him once since the day after she left. He walked into the house with her and settled down. Two days later Pamela was off again, and so was Tom. Next time we saw him was when Pamela came home for a brief holiday and found him waiting on the top step for her. They came in together, and again Tom settled down.

We were careful after that to look for Tom, but no one ever saw him except when Pamela came home again. Finally Pamela got married and moved away. Tom has never been seen since.

Now this is not someone's imagination playing games. Nor do we have another Clothild here. There was no evidence whatever that any other home was being used—Tom gave every indication of living a feral existence when he wasn't with us—or rather, with Pamela. There were six witnesses to Tom's comings and goings and his flawless timing. How in heaven's name did that cat know in advance that Pamela was coming home?

Pamela, we know, is a true animal person. She communicates with animals on a far more sophisticated level than most of us. In Africa once, on safari, she talked a wild genet (a relative of the mongooses) out of a tree and within four hours had it standing on its hind legs with its forepaws on her knee while it accepted food from her fingers. Could she have an aura that moves on ahead of her? One that alerted Tom that she was coming? O.K., I agree, that is voodoo nonsense. So let me hear your explanation.

Omari is an interesting marmalade-and-white cat who came as a truly wild monster. He was born to a feral mother (feral really has two applications: to children who have been raised by wild animals, as Romulus and Remus, and to such plants and animals as were once domesticated but have returned to a wild way of life—i.e., apple trees or cats, strawberries or dogs). When Omari was found he could not be handled. He scratched and screamed and bit. He appeared to be a hopeless case, but, again, a cat turned a corner and liked what he found. He is still nervous about being picked up and restrained, but he will snuggle beside you on a couch and he loves to be petted. Omari found us and evidently decided that it was better to lick than scratch the hand with the food, the hand that turns the knob to where it is warm and cozy and free of danger. Just another ill-starred cat who lucked in.

Although every single cat that has come and gone with

us has a story of its own, we don't want to run the risk of compiling a catalog. For every cat I have mentioned, however, there have been a couple more, at least. Some were short-term visitors, others lived on and finished their lives with us. There are only three more I would like the privilege of including, a cluster of incredible beauties—a bouquet of cats, if you will.

We had never had a litter born to us in thirty years of marriage, and we had bought very few cats. Virtually all of the cats we had taken on had been rescue cases, and I thought it might be fun at least once to start from scratch (so to speak). While shooting a television story about feline leukemia, I visited the cattery of one of America's leading cat judges, an expert named Richard Gebhardt. For twelve years Dick was president of the CFA—Cat Fanciers Association. He lives in Denville, New Jersey, with some of the most beautiful cats in the world, for he is a breeder as well. (He is also into dogs, toy English spaniels.) He showed me some of his incredible creations, and one evening soon afterward I returned with Jill. After a cup of coffee with Dick, we went into the cattery. He had several adults and a litter of what I think is the most exquisite of all American shorthairs, the silver ash tabby. It is difficult to describe this cat. It has two colors, glistening midnight black and silver ash, which is rather like a newly minted silver coin. The markings are prescribed by the standards. On each side there is a silver whorl that ends in a large black bull's-eye, and there are black necklaces on a silver ash background, at least one of which must be perfect and unbroken. The legs are horizontally striped. There is a series of marks including an M on the forehead. Silver ash tabbies tend to have round little faces and are quite small. In fact, they are like gems, and when people see them for the first time they usually are amazed at their perfection, if the cats are good examples of the breed.

Dick Gebhardt had good ones in his litter; they were just about perfect, and although most had been spoken for long since, he could spare one baby queen, to which we immediately attached ourselves. And so we got Maridadi. Maridadi is Swahili for beautiful, and since we had spent a month in Africa every year since 1971, a Swahili name seemed in order.

Dick warned us of one problem with silver ash tabby American shorthairs. They have very small litters. It is not unusual for a queen to have one kitten or two. Some lucky breeders get three, and there was a record somewhere of one cat that had five at one time.

In time little Maridadi became a fully grown splendid jewel, and she went to her first show. She got four ribbons, and figuring that was probably as many as we needed in the drawer with scores and scores of dog-show ribbons, we decided that her first would also be her only show.

When Maridadi was of age, just under a year, she went back to Dick's New Jersey cattery to be bred to an outstanding male of Dick's choosing. After she came back we all hoped "it had taken," as people say in the animal world. It had, oh, my, how it had! Dick had warned us again about the small litters, and since first litters tend to be even smaller than average we waited patiently just over two months for our one or two kittens. We did comment from time to time that Maridadi had apparently taken up her African name because clearly she was going to have a litter of one or two rhinoceroses. She got bigger and bigger until she could barely walk. By nature a very small cat, she was stretched to the size of the Goodyear blimp.

When the event seemed imminent, we moved a large crate into our bedroom and gave Maridadi all the comforts she could want to make it truly her confinement. With so many other animals around we thought it better that she be given privacy rather than find it for herself in the linen closet or under a couch, where other cats could still bother her with their curiosity. During the day she had the run of our bedroom with the door closed. At night she was crated.

Jill woke me very early the second morning of the confinement: "There's a kitten." Unfortunately the kitten, which had appeared while we were asleep, was dead. "Wait," Jill said, "there are two more." Maridadi continued to deliver kittens until noon. She had nine. We called Dick Gebhardt and could hear him suck in his breath on the other end of the line. "Nine," he gulped, "only you could have nine in a litter of silver tabbies!"

With a litter that large, some young are bound to be cheated *in utero*, and indeed three were born without their sucking reflex sufficiently developed. We did everything possible to feed them short of tube feeding. With animals that small—and these were absolutely tiny, each weighing barely as much as a tablespoon of sugar—getting a tube into the stomach without doing damage there or getting into a lung is virtually impossible. To feed three animals this way every few hours night and day and not have accidents is too much to hope for. So we did not tube-feed them. We did put them on their mother time and again, and we tried bottles and eyedroppers, but the three didn't yet know how to swallow, and by the second afternoon they had mercifully died without being aware enough to really suffer. We were left with five positive brutes.

The very smallest of all, the inevitable runt, was the one we decided to keep. We named him Siafu, which is the Swahili name for a tiny species of biting ant. On his second day Siafu developed an open sore on his shoulder. It is possible that Maridadi, not at all experienced in mothering, may have punctured his tender hide while moving him around. An infection quickly developed, and when he was only three days old tiny Siafu, the runt, had to have surgery. Fortunately Clay was home from medical school with some friends, one of them a very nice girl who was also about to be a doctor. Together, using a small syringe, they irrigated the wound every few hours, and on a heavy dose of antibiotics the poor little kitten, who had yet to see the light of day, made it. The last thing the two medical students did before they had to leave and get back to the hospital in Boston was extract a promise. It appeared as if there might be joint damage. If it was bad enough, we agreed, we would have the leg amputated at the shoulder and Siafu could make it as a three-legged cat. We had to promise not to have him destroyed. One or the other of them—as if that would have been necessary—would take responsibility for him. Well, Siafu did have joint damage, and today he has a somewhat wonky leg, but he is fine—no longer the runt, and so spoiled it just isn't believable. He loves to be picked up and carried—harking back, no doubt, to the weeks when he was carried and treated and hand-fed and given medication—those few first weeks of his life. Now if he will only stop climbing people as if they were telephone poles, everything will be fine.

Three of the litter went out at eight weeks, two of them to television producers I work with and one to a veterinarian. There were plenty of other takers lined up. The last kitten, not counting Siafu, was a large roly-poly female we called Safari. She and Siafu were such fun together that on the last day before she was to leave Jill looked at me and I looked at Jill—that certain look that has always said, without words "... so what is one more?" And I did a terrible thing. I called the potential buyer and told her that all the kittens had developed runny noses and none could leave for a while. It was an out-and-out-lie, but we never heard from her again; and Safari, much larger than her brother, has grown up to be even more magnificent, if possible, than her mother, Maridadi the beautiful.

Both Jill and I had worked so long in humane education and in rescue work that we felt guilty about producing even so splendid a litter of kittens. We have justified it in several ways, of course. After a lifetime of rescuing animals, after endless contributions to get cats and dogs spayed, Bastet owed us a litter. Another even better justification illustrates a basic truth about cats and dogs. They are short-lived, and if all the breeding of even the finest specimens stopped, all of those breeds that represent thousands of years (almost four thousand in the case of cats, and perhaps as many as twenty thousand in the case of dogs) of work and love and dedication would become extinct within two decades. This is true—in twenty years, all breeds of dogs and cats would be gone forever if the very best were not selected and bred to the very best by plan at measured intervals. And Maridadi is one of the very best.

Safari and Siafu may be the most technically beautiful or perfect cats we have ever owned, and they may be just about the cutest creatures on earth. But it took a long time to get them, and by no means are they loved more than the others.

Our lives have been full. A couple of splendid kids, a granddaughter, lots of dogs and horses and other animals, loads of acquaintances, some very good friends, travel almost without end. I have been abroad over fifty times in pursuit of material for my books and television, all fifty states, most of Canada, much of Mexico. Art, music, theater, wine, food, all the really good, fulfilling and exciting things in life. If today I were asked to state my complaints, I don't know that

I could in good conscience find anything to complain about. But it is also true that life would not have been as good and interesting, and would certainly have been missing some tranquil moments, along with more laughs than I can count and more qualities than I can identify, if it hadn't been for the cats in our lives. They are not better than dogs in any way I can name, and they certainly haven't replaced people, or even books and art. But they are cats, distinctly wonderful creatures that make and fill and possess forever a place in the hearts and minds of the people who are fortunate enough to come to know them. I am grateful for every one of them, as I am sad for all those others we could not really get to know. For if truth be told, and however impossible the idea, I would like to have known every cat that has ever lived.

Study by Kuniyoshi

Bibliography

THERE ARE HUNDREDS OF BOOKS ON CATS IN THE ENGLISH LANGUAGE. A
COMPREHENSIVE BIBLIOGRAPHY IS MORE THAN IS CALLED FOR HERE BUT PEO-
PLE INTRIGUED BY THE SUBJECT MAY FIND THESE BOOKS USEFUL, OR AT LEAST
ENJOYABLE. IN A VERY REAL SENSE THIS IS A SKELETON FELINE BIBLIOGRAPHY.
THIS LIST, IN TURN, CAN LEAD THE EXPLORER DEEPER AND DEEPER INTO THE
SUBJECT.

Allaby, Michael. *Your Cat's First Year*. New York: Simon and Schuster,
1985.
Caras, Roger. *Harper's Illustrated Handbook of Cats*. New York: Harper &
Row, 1985.
Carlson, Delbert G., and Giffin, James M. *Cat Owner's Home Veterinary
Handbook*. New York: Howell, 1983.
Carr, William H. A. *The New Basic Book of the Cat*. New York: Scribner's,
1978.
Dale-Green, Patricia. *Cult of the Cat*. Weathervane, 1963.
Gebhardt, Richard. *A Standard Guide to Cat Breeds*. New York: McGraw-
Hill, 1979.
Grilhe, Gillette. *The Cat and Man*. New York: Putnam, 1974.
Guggisberg, C. A. *Wild Cats of the World*. New York: Taplinger, 1975.

Hart, Ernest H., and Hart, Allan H. *The Complete Guide to All Cats*. New York: Scribner's, 1980.

McGinnis, Terri. *The Well Cat Book*. New York: Random House, 1975.

Mery, Fernand. *The Life, History and Magic of the Cat*. New York: Grosset & Dunlap, 1966.

Pond, Grace. *The Arco Book of Cats*. New York: Arco, 1970.

————, Ed. *The Complete Cat Encyclopedia*. New York: Crown, 1972.

————, and Calder, Muriel. *The Longhaired Cat*. New York: Arco, 1975.

Randolph, Elizabeth. *How to Be Your Cat's Best Friend*. Boston: Little, Brown, 1981.

Siegal, Mordecai, Ed. *Simon & Schuster's Guide to Cats*. New York: Simon and Schuster, 1983.

Suares, Jean-Claude. *The Indispensable Cat*. New York: Stewart Tabori & Chang, 1983.

Van Vechten, Carl. *The Tiger in the House*. New York: Alfred A. Knopf, 1950.

Wilbourn, Carole C. *The Inner Cat*. New York: Stein & Day, 1978.

Wolfgang, Harriet. *Shorthaired Cats*. Jersey City: TFH Publications, 1963.

Wright, Michael, and Walters, Sally, Eds. *The Book of the Cat*. New York: Summit Books, 1980.

Glossary

ABDOMEN: the belly; the trunk below or behind the chest

ACA: American Cat Association, the oldest governing body in North America

ACFA: American Cat Fanciers Association

AGOUTI: a coat pattern in which the individual hairs are banded with different colors. Example: Abyssinian cat.

AILUROPHILE/PHOBE: cat lover/hater

ALBINO: an animal lacking pigmentation in the hair and skin. The eyes are usually pinkish.

ALTER: a neutered or spayed cat

ANESTRUS (ANOESTRUS): the time between the sexually receptive periods of estrus

ANGORA: the name originally given to cats with long fur in Europe, so called after Angora (now Ankara) in Turkey, from where they were thought to have come. Now a recognized breed.

ANTIBODY: a substance produced by white blood cells in response to "foreign" protein, such as that of a bacterium. Helps to neutralize and fight the invasion.

AOC: any other color—that is, any color other than those specifically recognized in a breed

AOV: any other variety—that is, any pedigree cat not specifically recognized as a member of a breed

ATAXIA: staggering, usually resulting from an ear or brain disorder

BACK-CROSSING: mating a cat back to one of its parents

BARRING: a striped pattern, a form of tabby marking; a fault in self-colored cats

BC GENERATION: back-cross generation, the results of back-crossing

BICOLOR: having a patched coat of white and another color

BLAZE: a very light—usually white—marking running from a cat's forehead to its nose

BLOODLINE: a "family" of cats related by ancestry or pedigree

BLUE: coloring ranging from pale blue-gray to slate-gray

BREED: a group of cats with similar, defined physical characteristics and related ancestry

BREED TRUE: to produce a kitten exactly the same as the parents

BRINDLING: hairs of the wrong color mixed in with those of the correct color

BRUSH: a bushy or plumelike tail on a longhaired cat

BUTTERFLY: the pattern of markings seen on the shoulders of well-patterned tabbies

BUTTON: a white or contrasting color patch anywhere on the body

CALICO: American term for tortoiseshell-and-white color combination

CALLING: repetitive cries by a female cat in season; this sound attracts the attention of toms and signals the female cat's readiness for mating.

CAMEO: chinchilla, shaded or smoke with red or cream tipping on the hairs

CARRY: in genetics, to possess a recessive gene that is not apparent in the phenotype but can be passed on to offspring. With reference to disease: to show no symptoms but able to pass the disease on to other animals.

CASTRATION: neutering of a male

CAT FANCY: a term used to refer to pedigree cats and their breeding, cat clubs and societies

CATNIP: a perennial plant (Nepeta cataria) whose smell gives most cats great pleasure

CATTERY: any place where cats are kept; in North America, a breeding establishment

CCA: Canadian Cat Association

CFA: Cat Fanciers Association, the largest American cat association, also encompassing Canada and Japan

CFF: Cat Fanciers Federation (USA)

CHAMPAGNE: American name for the chocolate color in Burmese and the lilac color in Tonkinese

CHAMPION, GRAND CHAMPION: awards for excellence given after success at a number of cat shows

CHARACTERISTICS: distinguishing features in the standard of points for which marks are awarded

CHINCHILLA: coloring in which only the outermost tips of the hairs are colored black or another color, the rest being white or pale

CHOCOLATE: medium to pale brown; in Siamese, distinctly paler than seal
COBBY: a low-lying body on short legs
COLOSTRUM: the first "milk" produced by the queen
CONDITION: general health and fitness
CONFORMATION: the particular body form of a cat, encompassing size, shape and characteristics of a breed. Also called "type."
CONGENITAL: describes a disorder arising before birth, either hereditary or due to abnormal development in the womb
CROSS-BREED: the mating of two pedigree varieties
CRYPTORCHID: a male cat whose testicles have not descended
DAM: mother
DEGENERATION: deterioration of an organ or tissue structure due to disease, old age or accident
DENSE: thick, full—to describe coat
DIFFERENTIATION: the process during an embryo's growth in which unspecialized cells develop into tissues and organs
DIGITIGRADE: walking on tiptoe
DILUTE: a paler version of a basic color, such as blue, lilac and cream
DILUTION: variation in color producing a weaker shade in the coat
DOMINANT: said of characteristic seen in the first generation of breeding although inherited from only one parent
DOUBLE COAT: fur with a soft undercoat and a thick topcoat of long hairs over it, as in the Manx
EGG CELL (OVUM): the female germ or reproductive cell
ENTIRE: not neutered
ENZYME: a chemical substance produced by the body that causes a chemical change of some kind, such as the digestion of food
FELINE: of the cat family
FeLV: feline leukemia virus
FERAL: describing a once domesticated plant or animal (or its descendents) living wild
FERTILIZATION: the union of a male sperm and female egg to form a single cell from which an embryo (and thence kitten) will develop
FETUS (FOETUS): an unborn kitten after differentiation of the organs and tissues. From this time, about four weeks after fertilization, growth consists mainly of an increase in size.
FIA: feline infectious anemia
FIE: feline infectious enteritis, also known as panleukopenia (FPL)
FIF: Federation Internationale Feline, the main cat fancy organization on the European continent, also encompassing associations on several other continents. Formerly the Federation Internationale Feline d'Europe (FIFE).
FIP: feline infectious peritonitis
FOLLICLE: the "pit" in the skin from which a hair grows; the sac in the female's ovary in which an egg develops
FPL: feline panleucopenia
FRILL: hairs framing the head in longhaired cats, also called the "ruff"

FROSTPOINT: American term for lilac (lavender)

FUR BALL: fur swallowed by a cat when cleaning itself that may form a feltlike mass in the stomach

FUS: feline urological syndrome

FVR: feline viral rhinotracheitis, the more serious of the two viral causes of feline respiratory disease

GCCF: Governing Council of the Cat Fancy, the body controlling cat shows in Britain

GENES: units of heredity, which control the growth, development and function of all organisms

GENETICS: the study of heredity

GENOTYPE: the set of genes an individual inherits from its parents

GESTATION: pregnancy

GLOVES: white patches on the feet, as seen in the Birman

GHOST MARKINGS: faint tabby markings seen in some (solid) colored cats, especially when young

GRAND PREMIERE: the equivalent of a Grand Champion for a neutered or spayed cat

GUARD HAIRS: long bristly hairs forming the outer coat

HAW: transient third eyelid, or nictitating membrane

HEAT: a term used to describe a female cat in season; when the female is ready to accept the male for mating

HEMATOMA: blood-blister

HEMOGLOBIN: the red coloring matter of blood

HEMORRHAGE: bleeding

HONEY MINK: the name given to the intermediate brown color of the Tonkinese, corresponding to chocolate

HORMONE: a chemical messenger secreted into the bloodstream by a gland in order to affect another part of the body

HOST: the animal upon which a parasite lives

HOT COLOR: overly reddish shade in cream-colored cats

HYBRID: a type of cat which results from mating one breed to another

ICF: Independent Cat Federation (USA)

INFERTILE: unable to breed

INTERBREED: the mating of two closely related cats such as mother and son, or brother and sister

INTERMINGLED: fur of two colors mingled together; required in the blue-creams

KINK: a malformation of thickening of a joint in the tail

KITTEN: a cat up to the age of nine months in Britain or eight months in the United States

LACES: white markings rising from the paw on the back of the rear legs

LACTATION: milk production

LAVENDER: American term for lilac

LILAC: pale pinkish-gray, known in North America as lavender

LITTER: (1) kittens born to a female cat at the same time; (2) clay granules, sand, etc., used to fill a sanitary tray

LOCKET: a white or contrasting-color patch under the neck

LONGHAIRS: a term used in Britain and other countries for all cats with long fur

LORDOSIS: the crouched, sexually receptive position assumed by a queen in estrus

LYNX POINT: American name for tabby point

MASK: the darker coloring in the face on cats with a pattern of contrasting points, such as the Siamese

MELANIN: the main pigment that gives color to skin and hair

MELANISM: having a very dark or black skin and coat

MITTENS: white patches on the front of the paws

MOGGIE: a mongrel cat

MONGREL: a cat of unknown but apparently mixed origin

MONORCHID: a male cat with only one testicle descended

MUTANT: an offspring which shows a genetic change from its parents; can be a random occurrence. Mutants can also result from exposure to radiation.

MUZZLE: the projecting jaws and nose of a cat

NATURAL MINK: the name given to the darkest color of Tonkinese, corresponding to seal-point Siamese and brown (sable) Burmese

NCFA: National Cat Fanciers Association (USA)

NEUTER: a castrated male cat or kitten

NICTITATING MEMBRANE: the haw, or third eyelid

NOCTURNAL: active at night

NOSE LEATHER: the skin of the nose

NZCF: New Zealand Cat Fancy

ODD-EYED: having eyes of different colors, usually one blue and one orange or copper

OLFACTORY MUCOSA: the area of the nose responsible for the detection of smells

ORIENTAL: the name of specific shorthaired varieties; also the shape of some cats' eyes

PADS: the cushions on the soles of the paws

PANLEUKOPENIA: another term (preferred in North America) for FIE (feline infectious enteritis)

PARASITE: any animal or plant that lives in or on another (the host), from which it obtains food and to which it usually does considerable harm

PARTICOLORED: a cat with a coat composed of two distinct colors, a bicolor

PATCHED: said of fur that has patches of different coloring, as the tortoiseshell-and-whites

PEDIGREE: a genealogical table recording ancestry

PENCILINGS: the delicate, pencillike markings on the faces of tabbies

PERSIAN: a type of cat which is also known as a longhair

PEWTER: British name for shaded silver

PHEROMONE: a chemical substance released by an animal that influences the behavior of another individual of the same species. Pheromones are involved in territorial spraying and sexual attraction.

PIEBALD: specifically black-and-white, but also applied to white spotting combined with other colors

PIGMENT: coloring matter

PINKING UP: a mainly British term for the characteristic coloring of the queen's nipples about three weeks after mating

PINNA: the ear flap

PLATINUM: the American name for lilac (lavender) coloring in the Burmese

POINTS: darker-colored areas on the head, ears, legs and tail, as in the Siamese

PREFIX: registered name of a cattery used before the names of all kittens and cats bred there

PREMIERE: a neutered or spayed cat that is equivalent to a male or female champion, having won its title in the same way

PRICKED: ears that stand upright and high

PUREBRED: with parentage and ancestry of the same variety

QUEEN: a female cat used for breeding

RANGY: long-limbed and long-bodied

RECESSIVE: to describe a characteristic which is passed on from one generation to another, but which may not necessarily show in the first generation

RECOGNITION: acceptance by the governing body of a cat association of the standard, describing a new variety of cat

REGISTRATION: recording the particulars of a cat's birth and ancestry with an official body

ROMAN: describes a nose with a high, prominent bridge, characteristically seen in some Siamese

RUFF: *see* Frill

RUMPY: a completely tailless Manx cat

RUSTINESS: a reddish-brown tinge in the coat of a black cat

SABLE: American name for brown, the darkest coat color, in the Burmese

SEAL: the dark brown found at the points of the darkest variety of Siamese

SEASON: the mating season, the time when a female cat is in estrus and ready to accept a mate

SELECTIVE BREEDING: breeding by planned matings between individuals with behavioral or physical characteristics that the breeder wishes to perpetuate and enhance

SELF, SELF-COLOR: the same color all over, without markings; also known as "solid-color"

SHADED: coloring in which the tips of the hairs are colored, the rest being white or pale, the tipping being intermediate between the chinchilla and the smoke

SHADING: gradual variation in coat color, usually from back to belly

SHOW STANDARD: a description of the ideal cat of a particular breed, against which actual cats are judged

SILVER: term applied to shaded silver and silver tabby, both tipped colorings

SIRE: father

SMOKE: coloring in which most of the hairs are colored, the roots being white or pale

SNUB: the short noses seen in some of the longhaired varieties
SOLID: American term for self
SPAYING: neutering of a female cat
SPOTTING: the occurrence of white patches in the coat
SPRAYING: marking with urine
SQUINT: cross-eyed, with the eyes so placed that they seem to look permanently at the nose
STANDARD, STANDARD OF POINTS: characteristics required for a recognized variety of cat and the ideal description of the variety against which cats are judged
STERILE: infertile
STOP: a break in the smooth line of the profile between the nose and the skull
STUMPY: a Manx having a stump of a tail instead of being completely tailless
TICKING: bands of color on a single hair; *see Agouti*
TIPPING: contrasting color on the tip of the hair, as in the Chinchilla
TRICOLOR: a cat whose coat is made up of three distinct colors
TUFTS: hair growing from the ears or between toes
UNDERCOAT: soft hairs that lie below the longer hair of cats with double coats
WEDGE: head shape seen in some foreign varieties
WHIP: a long, thin tapering tail, as seen in the Siamese
WHISKERS: the long bristles protruding from the cat's face

National and International Organizations and Publications

American Cat Association, Inc.
Althea A. Frahm, Secy
302B South Brand Boulevard
Glendale, CA 91204

American Cat Fanciers Association
Mrs. Cora Swan, Secy
Box 203
Point Lookout, MO 65726

Animal Protection Institute of
  America (API)
P.O. Box 22505
6130 Freeport Boulevard
Sacramento, CA 95822

Animal Welfare Institute
P.O. Box 3650
Washington, DC 20007

Canadian Cat Association
Mrs. Dorothy Lamb, Secy-
  Registrar
Suite 5
14 Nelson Street West
Brampton, Ontario

Cat Fanciers Association, Inc.
P.O. Box 430
Red Bank, NJ 07701

Cat Fanciers Federation, Inc.
Mrs. Grace M. Clute,
  Corresponding Secy
2013 Elizabeth Street
Schenectady, NY 12303

Cat Fancy
11760 Sorrento Valley Road
San Diego, CA 92121

Cats Magazine
P.O. Box 4106
Pittsburgh, PA 15202

Crown Cat Fanciers Federation
Mrs. Martha Rose Underwood,
  Secy
1379 Tyler Park Drive
Louisville, KY 40204

Federation Internationale Feline
Friedrichstrasse 48
6200 Wiesbaden
West Germany

Feline Association of South
  Australia
P.O. Box 104
Stirling
South Australia 5152

Friends of Animals, Inc.
11 West 60th Street
New York, NY 10023

The Fund for Animals
140 West 57th Street
New York, NY 10019

Governing Council of the Cat
  Fancy
Dovefields
Petworth Road
Witley, Surrey GU85QU
England

The Humane Society of the United
  States
2100 L Street, Northwest
Washington, DC 20037

The Independent Cat Association
211 East Olive
Suite 201
Burbank, CA 91502

Independent Cat Federation
Mrs. Carolyn Alig, Secy
3512 East Milton Street
Pasadena, CA 91107

Kensington Kitten and Neuter Cat
  Club
Fairmont
78 Highfield Avenue
Aldershot, Hants
England

National Cat Club
The Laurels, Chesham Lane
Wendover, Bucks
England

National Cat Fanciers Association,
  Inc.
Mrs. Frances Kosierowski, Secy-
  Recorder
1450 North Burkhart Road
Howell, MI 48843

The Nature Conservancy
1800 North Kent Street
Arlington, VA 22209

New Zealand Cat Fancy Inc.
P.O. Box 3167
Richmond, Nelson
New Zealand

Pet Pride
15113 Sunset Boulevard
Pacific Palisades, CA 90272

United Cat Federation
6621 Thornwood Street
San Diego, CA 92111

United Cat Federation, Inc.
Jean Ford, Secy-Recorder
6616 East Hereford Drive
Los Angeles, CA 90022

World Wildlife Fund
1255 23rd Street, Northwest
Washington, DC 20037

Organizations and Publications

(*categorized by breed*)

ABYSSINIANS

The Abyssinian Cat
2 1106 River Road
Marengo, IL 60152

Abyssinian Cat Club of America
Wain Harding
2425 Ashby Avenue
Berkeley, CA 94705

Abyssinian Society of the
    Northwest
Henrietta Shirk, Secy
601 Sierra Vista Road
Newberg, OR 97132

Canadian Association for the
    Advancement of Abyssinians
Ms. M. Baird, Secy
4185 Fieldgate Drive #92
Mississauga, Ontario L4W 2M9
Canada

BALINESE

American Balinese Association
R.D. 2, Box 164
Columbus, MS 39701

Balinese Breeders and Fanciers of
    America
Pat Horton, Secy
16532 Ballinger Street
Sepulveda, CA 91343

Balinese International
7219 Larchwood
Woodridge, IL 60515

Eastern Balinese Association
Gayle Dennison, Secy
M.R. 1 Clearview Road
Souderton, PA 18964

Eastern Balinese Mews
Route #2
Hawkinsville, GA 31036

Bali Tales
P.O. Box 11
Livermore, CA 94550

BOMBAYS

International Bombay Society
Patt Taylor
2741 E. Sylvia
Phoenix, AZ 85032

BURMESE

Sacred Cat of Burma Fanciers
211 Hull Avenue
Staten Island, NY 10360

United Burmese Cat Fanciers
Mrs. T. H. Griffey, Secy
14435 Chadbourne
Houston, TX 77079

United Burmese Cat Fanciers
2395 N.E. 185th Street
N. Miami Beach, FL 32604

CAMEOS

Cameo Cat Club
251 Dorsey Road
Rochester, NY 14616

CHARTREUX

Chartreux Cat Mews
5519 Chelsea Avenue
La Jolla, CA 92037

CHOCOLATE AND LILAC LONGHAIRS

United Chocolate and Lilac
    Longhair Society
253 Pond Street
Westwood, MA 02090

HIMALAYANS

Atlantic Himalayan Club
7908 Belmont
Ft. Pierce, FL 33450

Himalayan Society
Judy Twitchell, Secy
32 E. Center Street
Mohawk, NY 13407

The Himalayan Society
Judy Sporer, Secy
R.D. 1, Box 424
Mohawk, NY 13407

International Himalayan Society
11751 Ranchito
El Monte, CA 91732

JAPANESE BOBTAILS

Japanese Bob Tales
162 W. Hudson Street
Long Beach, NY 11561

KORATS

Korat Cat Fanciers Association
122-7126 N. 19th Avenue
Phoenix, AZ 85021

Mai Pen Rai (Korat Cat Fancy)
P.O. Box A
Moriches, NY 11955

Maine Coon Cat

The Maine Line
P.O. Box 1399
Chula Vista, CA 92012

Manx

American Manx Club
13 Merrywood Road
Wappingers Falls, NY 12590

Canadian Manx and Cymric
Society
1402 Bethany Lane
Ottawa, Ontario K1J 8P6
Canada

The Manx Cat
P.O. Box 20072
Bloomington, MN 55420

Manx International
2275 W. 25th Street #22
San Pedro, CA 90732

Persian

Sanguine Silver Society
966 Blue Ridge Avenue N.E.
Atlanta, GA 30306

Sanguine Silver Society
208 Caito
Columbus, OH 43214

United Silver Fanciers
8 Debra Place
Syosset, NY 11791

Rex

Rex Breeders United
Sheila McMonagle, Secy
414 Normandy Drive
Lansing, MI 48906

Scottish Folds

International Scottish Fold
Association
664 Valerie Drive
Newton Square, PA 19037

Shorthair

National Exotic Shorthair Club
P.O. Box 943
Deer Park, WA 99006

National Short Hair Club
1331 N. Wingra Drive
Madison, WI 53715

Oriental Shorthair International
2127 Ridge Street
Yorktown Heights, NY 10598

Siamese

National Siamese Cat Club
16 S. Court
Port Washington, NY 11050

The Siamese Cat Society of
America, Inc.
Sam L. Scheer, Secy
2588-C S. Vaughn Way
Aurora, CO 80014

Somalis

Somali Cat Club of America, Inc.
Evelyn Mague, Pres.
10 Western Boulevard
Gillette, NJ 07933

Tonkinese

Tonkinese Breed Club
156 Berkey Street
Waltham, MA 02154

Turkish / Angora

International Turkish-Angora Cat
  Club
P.O. Box 13737
Gainesville, FL 32604

Wirehair

American Wirehair International
4438 Woodland Brook Drive
Atlanta, GA 30339

American Cat Association (ACA)
Lois Foster, Pres.
P.O. Box 533
Georgetown, FL 32039

Canadian Cat Association
14 Nelson Street W., Suite 5
Brampton, Ontario, Canada

Cat Chat
Maryland Feline Society, Inc.
P.O. Box 144
Lutherville, MD 21093

Happy Household Pet Cat Club
439 Calle de Castellana
Redondo Beach, CA 90227

Happy Household Pet Club
3200 "C" Street
Sacramento, CA 95816

The International Cat Association
  (TICA)
Georgia A. Morgan, Secy
220 E. Arroyo Drive
Harlingen, TX 70808

Picture Sources

Study by Kuniyoshi

Index